Routledge Revivals

The Elements of Greek Philosophy

The Elements of Greek Philosophy (1922) is an overview of the basic principles of Ancient Greek philosophy, tracing the developments of Greek thought from Thales of Miletus to Socrates, Plato and Aristotle.

The Elements of Greek Philosophy
From Thales to Aristotle

R.B. Appleton

First published in 1922
by Methuen & Co. Ltd.

This edition first published in 2025 by Routledge
4 Park Square, Milton Park, Abingdon, Oxon, OX14 4RN

and by Routledge
605 Third Avenue, New York, NY 10017

Routledge is an imprint of the Taylor & Francis Group, an informa business

All rights reserved. No part of this book may be reprinted or reproduced or utilised in any form or by any electronic, mechanical, or other means, now known or hereafter invented, including photocopying and recording, or in any information storage or retrieval system, without permission in writing from the publishers.

Publisher's Note
The publisher has gone to great lengths to ensure the quality of this reprint but points out that some imperfections in the original copies may be apparent.

Disclaimer
The publisher has made every effort to trace copyright holders and welcomes correspondence from those they have been unable to contact.

A Library of Congress record exists under LCCN 22024833

ISBN: 978-1-032-90326-2 (hbk)
ISBN: 978-1-003-54710-5 (ebk)
ISBN: 978-1-032-90329-3 (pbk)

Book DOI 10.4324/9781003547105

THE ELEMENTS OF GREEK PHILOSOPHY

FROM THALES TO ARISTOTLE

BY

R. B. APPLETON, M.A.

LATE SCHOLAR OF CHRIST CHURCH, OXFORD, AND CLASSICAL MASTER
AT THE PERSE SCHOOL, CAMBRIDGE

ἐφ' ὅσον ἐνδέχεται ἀθανατίζειν

METHUEN & CO. LTD.
36 ESSEX STREET W.C.
LONDON

First Published in 1922

TO
THOSE MEMBERS OF THE SIXTH FORM
AT THE PERSE SCHOOL, CAMBRIDGE,
IN THE TEACHING OF WHOM THE WRITING
OF THIS BOOK ORIGINATED

PREFACE

AS its title implies, this book is intended as an introduction to the study of Greek philosophy, whether begun at the Universities or in our schools. That elementary philosophy makes an excellent school subject has long been a conviction of mine; the growing mind of an intelligent boy seizes upon it as upon nothing else; it helps to formulate his ideas to a quite remarkable extent, and forms an educational instrument the neglect of which in England contrasts very unfavourably with continental usage. If this neglect has been due, as I believe that it has, to the lack of a suitable book upon the subject, it is my modest hope that the present work will help forward the improvement of classical education in this country. At any rate it should enable a boy to take a more intelligent interest in much of his classical reading. Allusions to the early philosophers are common in many of the authors usually read in schools, but to most boys they are mere names. This book will serve to give some significance to those names, and should also make the reading of such dialogues of Plato as are likely to be read in school more readily comprehended by the class. In past years there has been in the teaching of classics a tendency to give an undue emphasis to the purely linguistic side of Latin and Greek, which is now being rectified by the more humanistic attitude of those teachers who are attributing a greater and greater importance to the content of these languages. I shall be gratified if these find my book of some service to them.

I hope also that undergraduates beginning the study of Greek philosophy will find my simplified exposition a real help towards the comprehension of more advanced works upon the subject. If they once grasp the general principles of the movement of thought involved, they will not have to worry their tutors for an explanation of elementary points to the extent which I myself did in my student-days. Remembering this I have attempted at the outset to give some idea, in language as simple as I could command, of what philosophy is. Then come two chapters dealing with the Ionian physicists and the Pre-Socratics, in dealing with whom my main desire has been simply to make the philosophical development, which they represent, clear enough to render Plato intelligible. At the same time I have tried to bring out the general significance of the philosophical positions, which they maintained, in such a way that the student will not lose sight of main principles amid a mass of details—will not, as we say, fail to see the wood for the trees. Moreover, as I wanted to make these philosophers *real* to the reader, and not a mere set of names upon which to hang this or that doctrinal "tag," I have recorded the gist of what we are told about them in the various classical authors—all of which has led to a somewhat more lengthy treatment than one would at first imagine to be necessary. After a chapter upon the Sophists, we come to the main body of the book in the two chapters upon Socrates and Plato. Here alone have I given translations from the ancient authors to any extent, because here alone are we dealing with an author who has a purely literary, as well as a philosophical, value. For the same reason I have given very few passages from Aristotle—they will just serve to give some idea of his style—but confined myself to an analysis (a very close one as regards the early books of the " Ethics ") of such teaching of his as is both intelligible to young minds and stimulating or helpful in the ordering of our thought.

I must here make what acknowledgment I can of my indebtedness to others. What I owe, especially in reference to the Pre-Socratics, to Professor Burnet's two books on " Early Greek Philosophy " and " Greek Philosophy from Thales to Plato " will be obvious to all who have read them. With regard to Plato I owe almost everything to Professor J. A. Stewart of Oxford, not only to his well-known books on " The Myths of Plato," " The Platonic Doctrine of Ideas," and " Notes on the Nicomachean Ethics," but also to the inspiration of his oral teaching. A similar acknowledgment is due, especially with reference to Aristotle and to the explanation of reality on page 107 to my former tutor, Mr. H. W. Blunt of Christ Church. Both of these have been so kind as to read through my manuscript, and I have gained immensely from their valuable suggestions and criticisms. My quotations from the fragments of the Pre-Socratics are, of course, taken from Diels' "Vorsocratiker." The Plato selections have been translated by my former pupil, Mr. D. M. Simmonds, now scholar of Christ Church, Oxford, but at the time a member of the sixth form at the Perse School, Cambridge, and I am pleased to have this opportunity of thanking him for the ungrudging way in which he has given me so much help. In particular I wish to thank Mr. A. Watson Bain, educational editor to Messrs. Methuen, and Principal H. J. W. Hetherington, University College, Exeter, the former for his most helpful and sympathetic advice, without which it is not too much to say that my book would never have been published, and the latter for his patient and discerning criticisms, without which the book would have been even more imperfect than it now is.

I gratefully acknowledge the kindness of the delegates of the Clarendon Press for permission to use the translation of Aristotle's "Metaphysics" by Mr. W. D. Ross in the Oxford Translations of Aristotle for the quotations in my last chapter. My thanks are also due to Messrs. Allen & Unwin for their kind permission to reprint William Cory's "Mimnermus in Church" from "Ionica," on page 156.

Although I have occasionally ventured to develop an idea of my own, and have attempted to bring out the significance of the different movements of Greek philosophical speculations in a manner which I have not seen so explicitly traced elsewhere, this publication does not imply any great claim to originality. I have written the book because I know of no other which treats the subject in a fashion simple enough to be understood by those whom I have had primarily in mind.

Finally, I should like to thank two of my friends, Dr. W. H. D. Rouse and Mr. H. Caldwell Cook, for their careful reading of the proofs.

R. B. A.

January, 1922

CONTENTS

	PAGE
INTRODUCTION—(a) What Philosophy is	1
(b) The theological conception of the universe .	7

CHAPTER

I. The Ionian Physicists and the materialistic conception of the
   universe 11
   (1) Thales of Miletus 13
   (2) Anaximander 15
   (3) Anaximenes 18
   (4) Heraclitus of Ephesus 20

II. The earlier Pre-Socratics—
    (a) The breakdown of materialistic monism . . . 23
        (1) Pythagoras of Samos 25
        (2) Xenophanes of Colophon 30
    (b) Eleatic monists—
        (1) Parmenides of Elea 32
        (2) Zeno 35
    (c) The discrepancy between Eleaticism and phenomena—
        (1) Empedocles of Acragas 37
        (2) Anaxagoras of Clazomenæ 39
    (d) The necessity for a theory of knowledge—
        (1) Atomism 42
        (2) Democritus as an ethical philosopher . . 44

III. The Sophists 45
     (1) Protagoras of Abdera 46
     (2) Gorgias of Leontini 48
     (3) Thrasymachus of Chalcedon 50
     (4) Euthydemus of Chios 51
     (5) The philosophical significance of the Sophists . 51

CHAPTER	PAGE
IV. Socrates and a theory of Conduct	54
V. Plato and the idealistic interpretation of the universe	69
General characteristics—Psychology—Politics—Myths—Doctrine of Ideas.	
VI. Aristotle and the teleological conception of the universe	113
Ethics — Politics — Psychology — Logic and theory of knowledge—Metaphysics.	
CONCLUSION—The conception of God, and the immortality of soul	152
APPENDIX—(a) Aristotle's criticism of Plato's Ideas	159
(b) List of technical terms with their philosophical meanings	163
INDEX—(a) English	167
(b) Greek	169

THE ELEMENTS OF GREEK PHILOSOPHY
FROM THALES TO ARISTOTLE

INTRODUCTION

(a) WHAT PHILOSOPHY IS

MOST of us have heard the expression *Take it philosophically*, and we understand the adverb to mean something like *with resignation*. It comes to have this meaning because to take a thing philosophically is to consider it as a whole, not as an isolated phenomenon peculiar to ourselves, but in comparison with the whole of our life and as something which might, and possibly does, happen to others as well as to ourselves. When a man realizes that a great personal calamity is not something peculiar to himself but common to the majority of his fellow-beings, in fact a strictly necessary or inevitable incident in human life as such, or when he succeeds in viewing it in relation to the whole of his many-sided, wonderfully endowed life, it no longer fills the whole of his mind and soul. In popular language we say that he has become more resigned to it and is taking it philosophically. Much of the philosophy of Epictetus[1] is directed towards inculcating this attitude of mind. He tells

---

[1] A lame Greek slave who gained considerable renown as a philosopher during the latter half of the first century under the Roman Empire. His pupil Arrian has preserved notes of his lectures for us.

us, for example, that a father should not say, upon the death of his child, that he has *lost* it, but rather that it is *given back*. By this he means to remind us that life is, as it were, the gift of the gods, and that only the usufruct of it, as lawyers would say, is really ours.

The Channels of Knowledge. We shall expect, then, to find that philosophy is concerned with viewing things in their context and with assigning a right value to them in relation to the whole of that context. Plato defined it as *a speculation upon all time and all existence* —θεωρία παντὸς μὲν χρόνου πάσης δὲ οὐσίας ("Republic," 486a). It is concerned with our knowledge as a whole; but before we can define it more precisely we must briefly consider how we come to have any knowledge at all. For man and beast alike the senses are the avenues through which comes knowledge of the external world. Sight, hearing, touch, taste, and smell are senses which we share with the lower animals. But man alone can draw general and universal conclusions from the *data* thus provided. Some animals—dogs, for example—are endowed with a further faculty beyond the sense-perception (αἴσθησις) which is common to the whole animal kingdom. They remember that the whip smarts, and are capable of visualizing the effects of turning the handle of a door. Roughly speaking, we may say that, in the scale of animal life,

αἴσθησις is common to man and beast, and that many animals have no other faculty;

φαντασία (visualization) and μνήμη (memory) are faculties which enable the more intelligent animals to acquire some experience of life (ἐμπειρία) which extends beyond the moment of sense-perception;

τέχνη (art or science) and λόγος (reason) are confined to man alone, and enable him to acquire scientific knowledge.

INTRODUCTION

Such knowledge is opposed to merely empirical knowledge, and we must first get this distinction clear. In the technical language of Aristotle we may say that scientific knowledge (ἐπιστήμη) is concerned not with particulars (τὰ καθ' ἕκαστα) nor even with generalities (τὰ ὡς ἐπὶ τὸ πολύ) but with universals (τὰ καθόλου). You will understand the distinction best by considering an example. I may know that, when my electric light suddenly goes out, it may come on again if I give the bulb a smart tap. Such knowledge is, for most of us, purely empirical, i.e. gained as the result of previous experience and not necessarily involving any clear comprehension of the reason. If I know that this reason is that a smart tap will probably cause a re-union of a severed filament, then my knowledge, however empirical it may originally have been, is now no longer purely so; and, if my tapping fails to restore the light, I shall understand that the lacuna was too wide to be bridged by such simple means. I must then call in the aid of the electrician with his scientific knowledge. My own empirical knowledge is, strictly speaking, concerned with particulars; it applies to my electric bulb, and when I pass on the tapping suggestion to a friend I have no confidence—presuming that my knowledge *is* purely empirical—that it will work with his. The electrician's knowledge, on the other hand, is scientific—it doesn't matter to him whether he is called in to see to my electric light, or to yours, or to anyone else's—and is concerned with *all* electric bulbs, i.e. not with particulars but with universals (τὰ καθόλου). It is opposed to empirical knowledge in that it investigates the universal *law* or *reason* that lies at the back of particular phenomena. In other words, it involves an act of reflection upon our sense-presentations, in virtue of which we are enabled to draw general conclusions—μία καθόλου ὑπόληψις ἐκ

Empirical and Scientific Knowledge.

πολλῶν τῆς ἐμπειρίας ἐννοημάτων, as Aristotle says. It is this that enables man to build up through a process of reasoning (λογισμός) an art or science (τέχνη), the possession of which distinguishes him from the lower animals.

The ὅτι and the διότι. The knowledge which this μία καθόλου ὑπόληψις entails is in some sense a knowledge of laws or universals. The scientist always wants to know the reason (αἰτία) of things; the empirical person only knows a fact (τὸ ὅτι), but the scientist asks why the fact is so; he tries to find out the cause (τὸ διότι) of each particular phenomenon. Empirical knowledge of the ὅτι apart from scientific knowledge of the διότι may, in certain circumstances, be dangerous. For example, an optician may prescribe wrong treatment of the eyes upon his empirical knowledge of the fact (τὸ ὅτι) that this or the other lens makes an improvement in the sight; whereas the oculist, who investigates the cause (τὸ διότι) of the impaired vision, may tell us that such a lens, although causing an immediate improvement in the sight, would in the long run prove very detrimental to the eyes. Every one will be able to think of further practical examples of the superiority of the knowledge of the διότι over that of the mere ὅτι.

Philosophy and Scientific Knowledge. Just as empirical knowledge is, strictly speaking, confined to this or that phenomenon, so scientific knowledge is confined to its own department. It deals with its "universals" only within this or that particular sphere—electricity, mathematics, or any of the applied sciences—but does not, as such, examine either the possibility or the validity of our knowledge of such "universals." It is, for example, quite beyond the sphere of physics to examine either how man came to formulate the "law of gravity" or what justification he has for believing in it. Logic, on the other hand, is a science which deals with the workings of the human mind, and—quite apart from this or that subject-matter—formulates laws for valid reasoning and examines the method by which conclusions may legitimately be drawn from given premises. It is a branch of philosophy in a sense in which physics is not. Metaphysics—as the name implies—comes after, and goes beyond, physics, because it takes the "universals" of physics, as of all other departmental sciences, and examines what claim they have to represent reality, or *to be true*. Philosophy alone can answer Pilate's question of "What is Truth?" and it is in this sense that philosophy has been called *scientia scientiarum*, the science of sciences, because it is, as it were, arbiter of the claims of specific sciences to represent truth. Scientific knowledge cannot determine this; it is confined to its own sphere, and cannot turn round upon itself in order to ask whence its knowledge comes. To do this is the chief function of philosophy—it has always to be asking "How do you know?" and it must give some explanation of the possibility of knowledge, and also some criterion by which to judge the claims of that "knowledge" to represent reality. A simple analogy will make this clear. We all know how old-fashioned people take the Bible for "gospel" (as we say), and how the uncritical person is inclined to take everything "in the paper" for truth—the fact of its being "in the paper" makes it true. Perhaps some day he will read an account of something of which he has first-hand knowledge, and will find such discrepancies between the newspaper's account and what he himself knows to have been the facts that henceforth his belief in the infallibility of "the paper" will be rudely shaken. Gradually he will come to realize that "the paper" is written by journalists of like passions with himself, and will begin to look for some other criterion

The Question of Validity.

of the truth of a statement beyond that of its mere appearance "in the paper." Similarly we realize, as we grow up, that a statement is not necessarily true *because* it is in the Bible; and it is the same with the whole of our knowledge. We cannot take it *upon authority*, either from another person or from a literary record. The examination to which we are thus led, of the criterion of truth, is the main business of philosophy, and is what is meant when it is said that philosophy alone can raise the question of validity. Such an examination will necessarily be a long and difficult one, and will take us far afield into the most abstract speculation. But certain common-sense rules may be laid down from the very beginning. We want, for example, the whole of the truth; "half-truths" are misleading enough in ordinary life, and will not do at all in philosophical speculation. We must consider every aspect of a thing and take every point of view into account. A bigot can see only one side of a question; he is certain that he is right and simply cannot see the other side, just as, in the old story of two knights coming upon a shield (silver on one side, and gold on the other) suspended from a pole, each knight was certain that the shield was of the colour which he saw so plainly before his eyes, and took his fellow for a liar and a knave, simply because he could not see his "point of view." Philosophy, on the other hand, will consider every point of view; as Aristotle tells us, its first concern is to consider αἱ πρῶται ἀρχαὶ καὶ αἰτίαι, and he defines these as four in number. They are:—

The Four "Causes."

ἡ οὐσία or τὸ τί ἦν εἶναι (formal cause).
ἡ ὕλη or τὸ ὑποκείμενον (material cause).
ἡ ἀρχὴ τῆς κινήσεως (efficient cause).[1]
τὸ οὗ ἕνεκα (final cause).

[1] It will be noticed that it is only in this third *cause* that the word is used in its usual or popular sense. In the other three cases the word

Every subject may be considered under any or all of these four causes, though some are more particularly concerned with one than with another. Tanning, for example, is concerned chiefly with leather, the material cause of a boot. But we may also consider a boot from each of the three remaining points of view. Its efficient cause is the labour and skill of the cobbler; its formal cause the general shape and design which makes it more suitable as a covering for the human foot than for a hand-bag; while its final cause is comfort in walking and the protection of the feet against the harshness of the weather and of the ground. The distinction between these four causes is a most important one; and the confusion of two of them is a frequent source of error. A certain type of scientific mind, for example, is inclined to think that the explanation of a thing rests in showing how it arose. But this, of course, gives only the efficient cause, and it may well be that the whole significance of the thing in question resides in its final cause. The reader will be able to think of examples for himself.

(*b*) THE THEOLOGICAL CONCEPTION OF THE UNIVERSE

Philosophy, as Aristotle said, begins in wonder. Man, as soon as he begins to reflect upon the world in which he finds himself, becomes conscious of the wonder of his environment, and asks himself how it all came there and what it means. Now this first attitude of reflection upon the external world is, strange as it may seem, a theological one; it peoples the universe with a host of θεοί external to man himself. Let us see how this arises.

Primitive man is conscious of himself as a living animal,

cause is used in a special philosophical sense to denote what in ordinary, everyday language might be called a *point of view*.

as a thinking person. His natural impulse, therefore, is to ascribe such personality to different aspects of the universe external to himself. And obviously these *powers* are much greater, and more sublime, than he is himself, for they are beyond his control and greatly transcend anything which either he or his fellow-man can achieve. One needs to be as mad as Salmoneus to attempt to imitate the thunder and lightning of Zeus. Of course, a developed theogony—such as that of which Zeus is at the head—does not suddenly spring into being. We are speaking for the moment of a stage of civilization prior to all this, and one of which our knowledge must, to a certain extent, be conjectural; but the science of anthropology has during recent generations taught us a great deal. Roughly speaking, there are two means at our disposal for studying the workings of the primitive mind :—

1. The early workings of the mind of a child.
2. The minds of savages existing to-day.

Animism. In both of these we find a tendency to ascribe life to what a more fully developed experience proves to be inanimate. Most little girls do so with their dolls, and imaginative children have been known to address lengthy monologues to the man-in-the-moon. So, to the savage, thunder and lightning are the manifestations of the wrath of a god, and if there is *one* unseen god in the universe—as thunder and lightning clearly prove—then why not *many* ? In fact there is no check upon the savage imagination, which quickly makes almost everything animate. This is what anthropologists call *animism*, because it is a belief according to which there is life or soul (*anima*) in everything, whether tree, river, or lake. The angry child who kicks the chair which hurt him is probably responding to the primitive instinct which made his savage progenitor people the world with the gods of his imagination. But, be this as it may, it is well established that animism was a very definite stage in the development of the human mind.

From this a systematic theology gradually arises: the sun, for example, is a god who drives his chariot daily across the heavens, the moon a goddess who reigns by night, and so on. In time—but not until the development of literature—a definite hierarchy is evolved, in which each god has not only his definite order but also his own peculiar functions: this is the god of healing, that the goddess of corn. These things are settled by poets gradually bringing order into the confused mass of oral tradition. Thus Herodotus tells us that it was Homer and Hesiod, for example, who first systematized the Olympian theology. "These are they," he says, "who formulated a theogony for the Greeks, and ascribed their names to the gods, and determined both their honours and their crafts, and made clear their types" (Herodotus, II. 53).

A Theogony.

In thinking of their gods the Greeks naturally visualized them as "supermen" in human form, which is what we mean by saying that Greek religion was anthropomorphic. Within this fully developed Olympian theology, as we may term it, it is very interesting to find distinct survivals of an earlier animism. Consider, for example, the "Metamorphoses" of Ovid. Stories such as those of Procne and Tereus, and the existence of hamadryads and nymphs of stream and lake, have no connexion with the hierarchy of Olympus, but are relics of a stage of belief prior to it.

Anthropomorphism.

But such an anthropomorphic theology, as this of the Greeks, is, like other human things, liable to decay; and we know that scepticism set in very early. Probably this was so as early as the time of Homer, who does not hesitate occasionally to exhibit the gods in a ridiculous light. Take, for example, the song of the bard Demodocus in the "Odyssey," which tells how Hephæstus cast his ἀράχνια λεπτά over Ares and Aphrodite in bed together, and then summoned the rest of the gods to mock at their plight: "And the gods, the givers of good things, stood upon the threshold, and unquenchable was the laughter that arose among the blessed gods as they beheld the devices of wily Hephæstus" ("Odyssey," VIII. 266 ff.). Such an episode would be impossible among a people who did not take their theology somewhat light-heartedly.

Before passing on to consider the effect of this scepticism upon what we have called the theological conception of the universe, perhaps it would be well to utter a warning against any possible misconception which might arise from the origin to which we have traced it. It involves no disparagement of later theological speculations. If an anthropologist tells us that our most treasured belief in immortality arises from the restless dreams of an over-gorged savage, who imagines that he sees the spirit of a dead friend come from the underworld to visit him by night, we ought not to be angry with our anthropologist, but to thank him for tracing the *origin* of the belief, even while insisting that his researches can contribute nothing to our conception of its *value*. To trace the origin of a thing is to consider its efficient cause (ὅθεν ἡ κίνησις) and has nothing to do with the valuation of the thing itself (τὸ τί ἦν εἶναι). To confuse these two aspects would be to confuse the efficient with the formal cause, against which we have already issued a warning.

CHAPTER I

THE IONIAN PHYSICISTS AND THE MATERIALISTIC CONCEPTION OF THE UNIVERSE

THE theological interpretation once discredited, we naturally get, by a swing of the pendulum, a materialistic one. Our consideration of this will be lengthy, and before we enter upon it we will say a few words about the long-established quarrel between religion and science. (Let the reader consider for himself how far this quarrel is due to a confusion of the *causes* which we have asked him to distinguish.)

Religious exposition has from the earliest times been in the hands of a priesthood; and a priesthood is naturally conservative. At Athens, for example, when the archons ousted the King, the King's priestly duties continued to be performed by a so-called βασιλεύς, who retained the royal title long after he had lost all his prerogatives except the priestly ones. But we need not multiply examples to prove that religion is conservative; the somewhat unenlightened attitude of the Church towards the discoveries of men like Copernicus and Galileo in the sixteenth and seventeenth centuries is sufficient proof of that. It was religious conservatism which made Aristophanes attack Socrates so mercilessly in the "Clouds." In his youth Socrates was much impressed by the physical speculations of Anaxagoras and others; but

Science and Religion.

12 THE ELEMENTS OF GREEK PHILOSOPHY

Aristophanes regarded all such speculations with disfavour, for they tended to displace the gods by materialistic abstractions, so that " The vortex reigns, after having driven out Zeus."[1] Such unenlightened opposition to scientific discoveries is, of course, no part of true religion. The pursuit of knowledge is ideally good, and there can be no opposition between truth and religion; but it needed a teacher like Plato, with his high conceptions both of knowledge and of religion, to convince men of this. But philosophy has a long way to go before it comes to Plato.

Scepticism, we have said, soon begins to have a disintegrating effect upon the early theological conceptions. It is felt that we cannot *know* anything about the gods; but we know water, fire, and earth when we see them. Let us confine ourselves to the known, or at least to the knowable, and leave the unknown and unknowable to take care of itself. Philosophy must concern itself with the material cause, with the ὕλη of things. This is various; but the conviction arises that underneath the many forms of matter, as known to us, there is one permanent ὕλη, which only changes its attributes—much as the ὕλη of water is the same both in steam and in ice. The first speculations of this nature were made by the early Ionian physicists of the School of Miletus.

Miletus. Miletus was in early days the most prosperous of the many Greek colonies settled on the coast of Asia Minor. The reasons for this were partly geographical and partly political. The hinterland of Asia Minor is a great table-land, or plateau, which was chiefly given up to sheep-farming; the wool was sent down the two great river valleys which

[1] Aristophanes, "Clouds," 828.

penetrate the interior, was dyed with the famous *murex* dye discovered by the Phœnicians, and then exported to all parts of the Mediterranean world. Miletus stood at the mouth of one of these two great rivers. This was in itself likely to give rise to great commercial prosperity, and it was enhanced by another factor. Miletus had early entered into an alliance with Alyattes, the King of Lydia, and this treaty was renewed with Crœsus. This freed the citizens of Miletus from all political fear of the too powerful neighbour at their back, and thus they were enabled to indulge in that leisure (σχολή) which is so necessary to culture.

1. THALES OF MILETUS

There are many scattered allusions in the classics to Thales of Miletus. We are told that he was one of the Seven Wise Men of antiquity; and he was evidently a figure that appealed to the popular imagination. We must distinguish this aspect of him from what we can determine about him as a philosopher. The story of his having fallen into a well while star-gazing [1] is probably apocryphal, and invented to illustrate the uselessness of σοφία; just as the other story about his having made a fortune through buying up all the olive-presses in Chios and Miletus, at a time when his knowledge of the stars warned him that there would be a great harvest of olives in the coming year, is an improving tale with the opposite moral.[2] But there can be no doubt that he was a man very different from our modern conception of a philosopher. Thus he was something of a military engineer, and accompanied Crœsus in that capacity upon his ill-fated campaign against the Medes. When Crœsus

---

[1] Plato, "Theæt.," 174a.   [2] Aristotle, "Politics," I. 11, 10.

was in difficulties about the crossing of the river Halys, it was Thales who hit upon the ingenious plan of cutting a canal to the rear of the army, thus making the river flow through two channels, which both became fordable.[1] He was also an astronomer, and his date is fixed by his having foretold the eclipse of the sun which put an end to the battle between the Lydians and Medes.[2] Modern astronomical calculations place this eclipse in the year 585 B.C. The theory which attributed the periodic rise in the waters of the Nile to the effect of the Etesian winds[3] was probably due to Thales; and certainly he was a politician of some repute. Thus we see him giving advice to the Ionians to make Teos their capital.[4] In fact, we know far more about him in these various aspects than as a philosopher pure and simple. All that we can say with certainty in this regard is that he taught :—

1. That water is the material cause of things.
2. That the earth floats upon water.
3. That everything is full of gods (πάντα πλήρη θεῶν).

That he should have chosen water as the one permanent ὕλη out of which all other forms of matter arise is very natural, for do we not see water in the three forms of a solid, a liquid, and a gas, in ice, water, and steam respectively? The second remark which is attributed to him, to the effect that the earth floats upon water, need not worry us. It does not seem to be of much significance, and is not inconsistent with the first statement; it is probably due to the contemporary conception of the world as a flat disk with Oceanus running around it. But the third statement, that πάντα πλήρη θεῶν, cannot be so easily dismissed. Of course

---

[1] Herodotus, I. 75.   [2] Ib., I. 74.
[3] Ib., II. 20.   [4] Ib., I. 170.

θεός does not imply personality; but, even so, how is this to be reconciled with the doctrine that the ὕλη of everything is water? What happens to this if everything is full of θεοί? The solution seems to be that this last statement was not part of the definitely philosophical teaching of Thales, but rather a wise saw attributed to him in his capacity of one of the Seven Wise Men. We may compare it with the statement, recorded by Aristotle,[1] that Thales maintained that the magnet possessed soul (ψυχή), i.e. life, because it attracted iron; and we must remember that Thales lived in an age impregnated with a belief in old nature-religion, which, though a considerable development of early animism, was quite of a piece with such remarks as this. It is, at any rate, quite inconsistent with his philosophical idea of materialistic monism, nor can we reconcile it by any conception on the lines of Virgil's *mens agitat molem*,[2] for that would involve a terrible anachronism in the history of philosophical development.

2. ANAXIMANDER

Anaximander also was a native of Miletus; he was born about 610 B.C., and was a pupil or associate of Thales. Like his master, he would seem to have been something of a scientist; Diogenes Laertius tells us that he invented the γνώμων, or index of the sun-dial; but, as it was known to the Babylonians before this time, it is probable that Anaximander merely introduced it to the Greeks from them. We are also told that he was one of the first to make a map of the world, and Hecatæus, the later geographer whom Herodotus loved so well, both used, and improved, this map. This is all that we can affirm with confidence about the

---

[1] "De Anima," 411a. [2] "Æneid," VI. 727.

personal life of Anaximander. In his philosophical significance he is the second of the great Ionian physicists. Thales had found the permanent ὕλη which underlies the manifold variety of phenomena, with which our senses present us, in water. But Anaximander seems to have felt a difficulty in deriving all phenomena from something which is itself *one of those phenomena*. Such a derivation looks like a combination of a conjuring trick with the fallacy which is known in logic as a vicious circle. If all phenomena arise from one permanent ὕλη and are merely different manifestations of it, surely this ὕλη cannot itself be one of its own many manifestations, but must be something over and above them, something which our senses, it is true, can present to us only in one or other of its manifestations, but which we nevertheless must not confuse with any one of them. This vague "something," which is thus posited at the back of phenomena, Anaximander called the Indeterminate or Infinite (τὸ ἄπειρον). This is the material cause of all phenomena, and all specific things arise from it and return to it. First of all by a process of separation, or ἔκκρισις, contrary pairs—such as *the wet, the dry*—are separated out (ἐκκρίνεσθαι). We must not think of this ἄπειρον as being in itself either wet or dry, or indeed as possessing any specific quality whatsoever. It is at once everything and nothing; for all possible "contrary pairs" are contained within it, not actually as such (ἐνεργείᾳ) but potentially (δυνάμει[1]), in that they are capable of arising from it. To give the ἄπειρον any definite quality would be to fall into the error of Thales and to make the permanent ὕλη of things itself one of the many

---

[1] This distinction between the *actual* and the *potential* is much later than Anaximander and comes from Aristotle, but it seems to be what Anaximander meant.

things which it has been brought in to explain. Moreover, if it were true, we should expect to find in the world a tendency for the different "elements" (earth, air, fire, and water) to vanish into one. But this is not so; they do not vanish into one of themselves, but only into the ἄπειρον from which they arose. Their specific qualities, while they exist, seem to have been regarded by Anaximander as a sort of violation of the neutral character of his ἄπειρον. One definite fragment of his writings has been preserved for us by Theophrastus; but it is in a form which makes it impossible for us to be certain of the exact words of Anaximander. It is as follows:—

ἐξ ὧν δὲ ἡ γένεσίς ἐστι τοῖς οὖσι, καὶ τὴν φθορὰν εἰς ταὐτὰ γίνεσθαι κατὰ τὸ χρεών· διδόναι γὰρ αὐτὰ δίκην καὶ τίσιν ἀλλήλοις τῆς ἀδικίας κατὰ τὴν τοῦ χρόνου τάξιν. Professor Burnet[1] takes the first clause as *oratio obliqua* (i.e. as the words of Theophrastus and not of Anaximander himself) and translates thus: "And into that from which things take their rise they pass away once more, as is ordained; for they make reparation and satisfaction to one another for their injustice according to the appointed time." It is difficult for us now to determine what induced Anaximander to conceive of the specific existence of things as an "injustice" (ἀδικία), but it seems reasonable to refer it to the advance which, as he thought, his philosophical system had made upon that of Thales by conceiving of the original "matter" out of which all things are evolved as not itself possessing any definite qualities. For this ὕλη to be determined in any one specific way is a sort of "injustice" to the numerous other ways in which it might have been determined.

[1] Burnet, "Early Greek Philosophy," p. 54.

Before we pass to his successor it should be stated that Anaximander seems to have had vague inklings of what nowadays we call the theory of evolution. If everything arises from the ἄπειρον, then, of course, man is included, and was once not as he is now, but has been gradually evolved. The reason which Anaximander gave as a proof that man was descended from other animals has a peculiarly modern ring about it. He says that, if this were not so, man could never have survived; the human child, compared with the young of other animals, needs such a lengthy period of suckling that it would have stood no chance of living, in the earlier and rougher days of the world, if it had always been such as we now know it.

3. ANAXIMENES

Anaximenes, the pupil of Anaximander, was another native of Miletus. His date is fixed for us by that of Anaximander, and we also have a *terminus ad quem* in the destruction of Miletus by the Persians in 494 B.C. The philosophical school of Miletus then came to an end, so we must put the *floruit* of Anaximenes before this date.

As with the other Milesians, the chief concern of philosophy is still, for Anaximenes, to determine the one permanent ὕλη from which all things arise. He taught that this was ἀήρ, and that things are evolved out of this either by a process of condensation (πύκνωσις) or of rarefaction (ἀραίωσις, μάνωσις). By ἀήρ we must probably understand something more akin to fire than to what we call "air," for in the process of ἀραίωσις fire is the next stage to ἀήρ, and in an example of πύκνωσις we find that ἀήρ is "rarer" than ἄνεμος (wind). We have "air, wind, clouds, water, earth, stones" in descending scale. Moreover, that it was hardly our "air" is probable from the remark of his that οἷον ἡ ψυχὴ ἡ ἡμετέρα ἀὴρ οὖσα[1] συγκρατεῖ ἡμᾶς, καὶ ὅλον τὸν κόσμον πνεῦμα καὶ ἀὴρ περιέχει· (As our soul, which is "air," holds us together, so the wind, and the "air," embraces the whole world.)

At first sight such a system as this looks like a set-back upon the advance made by Anaximander; the underlying permanent ὕλη is once more made, as it was with Thales, itself one of the specific things which arise from it. But it is not really so. It was only shallow thinking that made Anaximander find any difficulty in the derivation of all phenomena from something which is itself one of those many phenomena. It is difficult to realize how various phenomena arise from one permanent ὕλη, but that difficulty is not solved by the positing behind phenomena of some indeterminate element beyond those of earth, air, fire, and water.[2] If everything is derived from one material principle, it makes no difference to the plausibility of the derivation however we may conceive of that material principle. And whatever these early philosophers may have meant by "earth, air, fire, and water," it is highly improbable that they meant what these words suggest to our senses. According to the theory of Anaximander everything is derived from the "Indeterminate;" according to that of Anaximenes everything is derived from ἀήρ (vapour? In Ionic Greek the word means *mist*). The two theories are equally plausible, especially if we do not allow ourselves to think of ἀήρ as air.

So far from denoting a set-back upon the philosophical

[1] A common idea among the ancients.
[2] What are these four elements? It has been suggested to me by my friend, Mr. W. H. S. Jones, Fellow of St. Catherine's College, Cambridge, that they were a figurative way of speaking, that earth = solids, water = liquids, air = vapour, and that fire is something of the nature of vital warmth. And Dr. W. H. D. Rouse tells me that this is the sense in which these very names are used in Sanskrit philosophy.

system of Anaximander, the name of Anaximenes really marks a great step forward in the history of philosophical development. For in him we see the all-important idea of *process* rising into prominence in the functions which he assigns to πύκνωσις and ἀραίωσις. We are passing from a static to a dynamic conception of things, and the ideas which lie behind these two words are ideas which are destined to play a very important part in the development of philosophy.

4. Heraclitus of Ephesus

Although not of Miletus, Heraclitus really belongs to the Milesian school; for it is in him that we see the full exposition of that doctrine. He flourished about 500 B.C. or about the middle of the reign of Darius.

He wrote a book in a very obscure style, and considerable fragments of this are still extant. Without going into details of his many enigmatic sayings, we can piece together sufficient to obtain a fairly clear idea of his philosophical significance. He gives full expression to that doctrine of *process* which is involved, but not explicitly stated, in the early Ionian philosophy. Fire is the fundamental form of existence; but there is continual change going on—πάντα ῥεῖ. Fire passes by the ὁδὸς κάτω (cf. the πύκνωσις of Anaximenes) into water and earth; these, in their turn, pass by the ὁδὸς ἄνω (ἀραίωσις in Anaximenes) back again into fire. According to Anaximander the separating out of things from the ἄπειρον was regarded as a sort of ἀδικία, for which recompense has to be made. Heraclitus, on the contrary, regards the existence of the manifold of phenomena as a ἁρμονία of opposing tendencies such as that of the lyre and of the bow. It is, in fact, just this continual strife which makes the existence of the world possible. This idea is at the bottom of his doctrine of the unity of opposites and of the One and the Many.[1] "Life is death; sleeping is waking; we are and are not; young and old are the same." So runs a fragment which has been preserved in Plutarch. We must make allowances for poetical language, and also for that tendency to exaggerate which leads a great teacher or prophet to attempt to gain attention for his doctrine by making it as startling as possible. Such teaching must never, of course, be interpreted literally. There is a Christian precept which bids me take no thought for what I shall eat or what I shall put on; but, however good a Christian I may be, I shall not risk death from pneumonia by wearing the thinnest of my summer clothes in mid-winter, nor shall I, in reliance upon this precept, appease my hunger or thirst at random from the shelves of a chemical laboratory. We must interpret the seeming contradictions of Heraclitus in a like spirit; they are a symbolical way of asserting the relativity of things. Everything is relative to everything else; heat is impossible without cold, young without old, and so on. This interpretation fits in well with his fundamental doctrine of πάντα ῥεῖ, and is made certain by the words which immediately follow those just quoted, viz.: "For these by changing become those, and those again changing become these." Heraclitus calls them the *same*, because they so readily pass the one into the other. Change is, in fact, the great reality. This conviction lies at the bottom of all the speculations of Heraclitus; and if we wonder why he chose fire as the primary substance, it is probably not too fanciful to answer that he did so because a steadily burning flame, which looks

---

[1] The speculations of Heraclitus upon the One and the Many were purely physical. Later on they will have a very important logical application,

constant (though all the time "passing away") seemed to him the most stable thing in a world of continual flux.

The question with which philosophy started—What is the world made of?—has now been variously answered by Thales, Anaximander, Anaximenes, and Heraclitus. All these four philosophers concerned themselves primarily with the material cause of things; but we notice a gradual development, finally becoming explicit in Heraclitus, of the importance of the idea of *process* or *change*. The "how" gradually displaces the "what" in philosophical importance. The world may be made of earth, air, fire, or water; but we can rest satisfied with no explanation which does not account for *how* the different elements arise and pass into one another. Materialistic monism has failed to explain this " how," and materialism as a philosophy contains within itself its own refutation. It cannot account for motion, and motion is the great fact of life.[1]

[1] This criticism applies to the crudest form of materialistic monism such as that which we have just examined. Many shades of mechanistic explanation do not lie open to it in such an obvious manner, but to examine such later speculations here would be to obscure the great philosophical truth which has emerged as a result of this first great philosophical movement. The speculations of these Milesian monists may seem very crude when examined individually, but their philosophical importance lies in the course of speculation which they jointly represent—a course in which truth has, as it were, been working itself out. The details of their individual theories are of no significance as compared with the gradual evolution of philosophical truth to which each in his turn contributed. We have now reached the end of the first stage of that evolution, and if the reader has realized what this stage means he is beginning to understand the meaning of philosophy.

CHAPTER II

THE EARLIER PRE-SOCRATICS

(a) THE BREAKDOWN OF MATERIALISTIC MONISM

THE breakdown of materialistic monism marks the end of the first stage of Greek philosophical speculation. Of the four Aristotelian αἰτίαι or πρῶται ἀρχαί we have so far confined our attention to one, ἡ ὕλη. Subsequent speculation, though it does not confine itself definitely to any one of the remaining three, yet takes on a new aspect. This change coincides with a shifting of the scene of philosophical speculation from East to West. The Persian advance in Asia Minor must have made the Ionians feel the insecurity of their position for some time, and have induced them to turn their thoughts towards migration to the West. We know that this was actually suggested at least once[1] by Bias of Priene, who recommended that all the Ionians should set sail in a body and establish themselves in the island of Sardinia as a common centre for all of them. This, of course, was never achieved; but the Persian destruction of Miletus in 494 put an end to the philosophical school which had flourished there for so long: and we can imagine the philosophers escaping in various directions westward, just as the scholars fled to

Western Greece.

---
[1] Herodotus, I. 170.

different parts of modern Europe upon the sack of Constantinople by the Turks in 1453. Let us glance, then, at the conditions which obtained in the West at this time. Throughout Greece we find a sort of religious revival, although there has been no definite change in the State religion. As we have said, a priesthood is naturally conservative, and this is pre-eminently so in the case of an "established" priesthood, or State religion. But its influence was almost negligible in Greece and the Olympian theology had already lost what little appeal it ever had for the hearts of the people. The worship of Dionysus had been introduced from Thrace, and this with all its wild elements of romance, of fervour, and even of licence, soon took a firm hold upon those who found something lacking in the regular Olympian theology, something cold and, as it were, unreal. Then we have the Eleusinian and other mysteries, of which we know little. But there can be no doubt that they formed a very practical part of the religious life of the day; to some minds they would appeal most strongly owing to the sense of reality, almost of "earthiness," as seen in the significance given to vegetation and the return of spring after winter; to others of more mystical nature, they would appeal from the other aspect of all "vegetation cults," from what is symbolized by the re-awakening of all vegetable-life, i.e. the promise of life after death and the hope of immortality. It is probably this double appeal, this unusual combination of a spiritual and an "earthy" aspect, which accounted for the remarkable hold which the mysteries undoubtedly had upon the minds of many. Nor must we forget Orphism, and all those vagrant "medicine-men" and religious teachers of every description who would have a great influence, especially upon the less educated portion of a community.

Transplanted to such soil philosophy most naturally takes root rather as a *way of life* than as a body of academic doctrine. Religious brotherhoods spring up, and rules are formulated for the guidance of the initiated; one of the most famous of these is that which is associated with the name of Pythagoras.

Philosophy as a "Way of Life."

1. Pythagoras of Samos

Although a native of Samos, Pythagoras did not live there for the greater part of his life. He disliked the rule of Polycrates, who became tyrant in 532 B.C.—this fixes the date of Pythagoras—and emigrated from Samos to Croton in South Italy. Here he founded a religious brotherhood, which gradually became very powerful; there was definite teaching in connexion with it, and it seems to imply a school with an esoteric doctrine, into the full mysteries of which the novices were not initiated until after several years' service. The brotherhood established at Croton became powerful enough to get embroiled in political agitations. It was owing to some contest between it and the democratic party at Croton that Pythagoras had to flee the town and retire to Metapontum, where he died.

To most of us the name of Pythagoras at once suggests the transmigration of souls. We think of Shakespeare's suggestion that "the soul of our grandam may haply inhabit a bird." Classical students know that οἱ Πυθαγόρειοι is the way to translate "vegetarians." Let us begin with these two scraps of information. There is no shadow of doubt that the transmigration of souls formed part of the definite teaching of Pythagoras. It was a doctrine that appealed to the humour of the popular imagination, and Xenophanes (the next philosopher whom we shall consider) made fun of it thus :—

> They say that once as Pythagoras was passing by he took pity upon a dog that was being beaten and spoke as follows : "Hold, strike not! for it is the soul of a man dear to me, which I recognized as I heard its cry."

He is himself said to have believed that his soul formerly inhabited the body of Euphorbus, who fought in the Trojan war and dedicated his shield in a certain temple, where Pythagoras recognized it as the one which he had worn when Euphorbus.[1] The story makes us think at once of the doctrine of Recollection (ἀνάμνησις)[2] in Plato; but there seems to have been no systematic development in Pythagoras of the implications of this doctrine as regards a theory of knowledge. This belief in the transmigration of souls, or παλιγγενεσία[3] [μετεμψύχωσις is a later word, and not good Greek for it; it should, of course, mean not the passing of one soul into different bodies, which is what we want, but the habitation of a succession of souls in one body], is intimately connected with a belief in the kinship of man with the beasts, and with abstinence from flesh.[4] These always hang together, and the reason is obvious.

His Ethical Teaching. Beyond this more popular side of his teaching—was thus much the exoteric portion to which all members of the brotherhood were immediately admitted?—it is difficult to be confident that we are not going wrong in ascribing further doctrines to the personal teaching of Pythagoras. This difficulty arises from the confusion in our authorities between the doctrines of the immediate followers of Pythagoras and

---

[1] Horace, "Odes," I. 28, 10.   [2] See below, p. 109.
[3] See Ovid, "Metamorphoses," Book XV., for popular stories.
[4] Beans need not worry us here,

those of the later fourth century Pythagoreans. But we can conjecture something about the ethical teaching of Pythagoras himself, and there are indications that this was of a very high order. It is only natural now that philosophy is, as we have said, regarded rather as a way of life than as an academic body of doctrine, that ethical teaching should have played a very important, if not the most important, part in the training of the brotherhood.

The Aristotelian distinction [1] between the ἀπολαυστικός, the πολιτικός, and the θεωρητικὸς βίος (the life of pleasure, the "political" life, and the life of speculation) probably, dates ultimately from Pythagoras. For Pythagoras is said to have compared human life to one of those motley gatherings, of all classes of people, who assembled at Olympia to see the games; there are three classes of people who come: the lowest class is those who come to barter goods; the middle class those who come to compete in the games; while the highest class of all is that of the spectators. There are points here which are worthy of notice. The following of a trade was repugnant to the ideals of the Greek; he regarded it as something unworthy of a man with a soul above money-making. This was so at all times; how much more so, then, in the case of those who saw in a great national and religious festival nothing more than an opportunity for plying their own little private businesses to advantage?[2] Such people belong to the lowest stratum of humanity. It seems surprising, however, to find the spectators assigned to a higher class than the competitors. But the idea is peculiarly Greek; and we must not be prevented from appreciating it by any

---

[1] See below, p. 115.

[2] Compare Christ's indignation at the money-changers who turned His Father's house into a den of thieves.

analogies with the very different circumstances of modern times. We must not imagine that the spectators at the Olympic games were at all like the crowd at a modern football match. Public ceremonies were always for the Greeks occasions for the enjoyment of cultured conversation; and when Pythagoras compared such spectators with the highest type of human life, he was insisting symbolically that the highest activity of the human mind is disinterested speculation. Those who pursue knowledge for its own sake, without any ulterior motive either of gain or of renown, are surely following the highest ideals. We may conjecture, then, that the ethical teaching of Pythagoras involved a true estimate of the three " goods " of wealth or pleasure, of fame or renown, and of knowledge or wisdom; and such a doctrine will take one a long way in ethics.

The Doctrine of Numbers. There is a further doctrine which can be ascribed without doubt to Pythagoras himself. This is the doctrine of numbers, according to which *things* are said to be *numbers*. Baldly stated, it is a startling, if not an inconceivable, doctrine; and there are many fanciful developments of it, e.g. justice is defined as *four,* the first square number (ἀριθμὸς ἰσάκις ἰσός), because *four* so readily symbolizes the element of retribution (τὸ ἀντιπεπονθός) which constitutes an essential part of the popular idea of justice (ἅ τις ἐποίησεν ταῦτ' ἀντιπαθεῖν). Similarly *three* was marriage, the union of the odd and the even (male and female). But this is sheer symbolism. What induced Pythagoras ever to speak of things as numbers at all? There can be no doubt that he was much interested in the study of mathematics; it is recorded, for example, that he was the discoverer of the 47th Proposition of the first book of Euclid, and indeed some authorities ascribe most of that book to him. When we reflect upon it we realize that the idea of *number* is the one quality which is common to all things whatsoever—everything is qualified by it, and it forms a large element of the significance of very many things, of harmony and music, for instance. That number, proportion, design, form, and harmony are very important aspects of things all will admit. But to say that things *are* numbers, it may be objected, is a queer way of stating this truth. We must, however, remember firstly, that exaggeration and striking exposition are to be expected in the statement of a new doctrine,[1] and, secondly, that the use of the verb *to be* is peculiar in the history of philosophy. We shall find this cropping up again later.[2] Language has not yet distinguished between the meanings of *is identical with* and *is qualified by*, but uses the verb *to be* to denote both relations. So the true significance of the doctrine, that things are numbers, rests in its recognition of the *formal* aspect of things, of τὸ τί ἦν εἶναι as opposed to ὕλη.[3] Pythagoras would be an important figure in the history of philosophy if he had done no more than enunciate this one doctrine, for it draws attention away from the one aspect of things (the material one) to which previous philosophers had more or less confined themselves, and attracts it to another aspect equally or more significant. Form is more important than matter; we may have a very ugly and a very beautiful thing made of exactly the same material, and to consider nothing but the material of things is often to miss their most important qualities.

Before passing on from Pythagoras we ought to make

---

[1] Compare what was said above (p. 21) about the contradictions of Heraclitus.

[2] Cf. below, pp. 48, 107.

[3] See below (p. 162) the illuminating comment of Aristotle in "Metaphysics," 987b.

30 THE ELEMENTS OF GREEK PHILOSOPHY

Medicine and Music. mention of the importance both of music and of medicine in his teaching. Music is closely allied with "numbers" in more senses than one; the difference between musical notes, for example, is the difference between the *number* of vibrations that produce the note, and so on. But more than this; just as medicine is the purge of the ills of the body, so Pythagoras regarded music as the purge of the ills of the soul. Aristotle later on was to find in tragedy a κάθαρσις of the emotions, and similarly Pythagoras found a great ennobling effect of μουσική [1] generally upon the soul.

2. Xenophanes of Colophon

Xenophanes is sometimes regarded as the first of the Eleatic monists, who come next. But it is doubtful whether he ever went to Elea or not; so it is best to treat him as a precursor of that school. He precedes Heraclitus in time, but his philosophical significance is that of a precursor of a school of philosophy definitely opposed to Heraclitus' doctrine of the flux of all things. He lived as an exile for the whole of his life, and is dated by the fact that he dwelt for long at the court of Hiero of Syracuse, who reigned from 478 to 467 B.C. He wrote elegies and satires until the ripe age of ninety-two, and his philosophy is expressed incidentally in these poems.[2]

The most striking feature of his writings is a reaction against the anthropomorphic ideas of the gods made familiar

---

[1] The Greek word is, of course, of a wider connotation than its English equivalent.

[2] We have already seen an example of his satire in the lines upon Pythagoras. See above, p. 26.

by the older poets. Homer and Hesiod are especially blamed for this.¹

It is ridiculous of man to imagine that the gods are like himself; he is acting no more intelligently than cows or lions, who, if they represented gods, would make them in their own form. The Olympian theology, then, will not satisfy Xenophanes; but he does not follow that revival of the primitive elements of religion which made itself felt in the worship of Dionysus and in Orphism. He is, on the contrary, the first great monotheist; there is one supreme god, like man neither in mind nor in form, and we must not assign to him the limitations of human personality.² *Monotheism.*

This monotheism is intimately bound up with the general cosmology of Xenophanes; in fact θεός seems almost to be the universe. But it is not necessary for us to go into the details of his cosmology, since such speculations, after the Milesian School has served its purpose of showing the innate impossibility of materialism, are no longer our main interest in the history of philosophical development. But the idea of unity, which this monotheism involves, is very important. Aristotle says that Xenophanes was one of the earliest philosophers to insist on this—πρῶτος τούτων ἐνίσας (he was the first partisan of the One). By this is meant that he was the first to grasp the unity of existence, that there is order and system in the world, however much this may be obscured by the seeming conflict and differences between the manifold of

---

¹ "Homer and Hesiod," he says, "ascribed to the gods all things such as are held a reproach and a disgrace among men—theft and adultery and mutual deceit."

² "There is one God, the greatest among both men and gods, like unto mortals neither in form nor in thought; he is all seeing, all mind, and all hearing."

phenomena. The Many, that we see, is appearance; the One, that we don't see, is reality.

(b) THE ELEATIC MONISTS

1. PARMENIDES OF ELEA

Parmenides is by no means a mere name to us; he came to Athens, along with his disciple Zeno, in 450 B.C., and conversed with Socrates, who frequently went to see him in his lodgings in the Ceramicus outside the walls of Athens. Plato, in the dialogue called "Parmenides," has preserved for us so vivid a picture of this visit that we can easily visualize the pair—Parmenides already an oldish man of about sixty-five, quite white with age, but still handsome in features, Zeno almost forty and of a fine and comely figure. But we must, of course, be careful about attributing to the historical Parmenides anything which Plato puts into his mouth as a *dramatis persona* in his own dialogue; and there is a further difficulty in drawing conclusions from the actual fragments of Parmenides, which arises from the peculiar method which he adopted for expounding his philosophy. This was done in a long hexameter poem in two parts. After an introduction in which the goddess tells him of the "way of truth" and of the "way of opinion," we have the two ways expounded. There is no truth in the "way of opinion," but ignorant men wander along it in utter helplessness.[1]

In dealing with any fragment, then, it is of the first importance to determine whether it is a part of the way of

---

[1] "Mortals, knowing nothing, wander along it, facing both ways; for helplessness in their breasts guides their wandering mind, and they are borne along no less deaf than blind, bemazed, and indistinguishable crowds."

truth (τὰ πρὸς ἀλήθειαν) or of the way of opinion (τὰ πρὸς δόξαν). Even so, Parmenides is rather difficult to understand; but we shall get some help if we first attempt to view him in his philosophical setting.

The Pythagoreans, if not Pythagoras himself, seem to have regarded what we call reality as somehow consisting of a set of opposites, of antithetical pairs of things. Aristotle, in his "Metaphysics," has preserved a list of these as follows:—

πέρας	ἄπειρον	ἠρεμοῦν	κινούμενον
περιττόν	ἄρτιον	εὐθύ	καμπύλον
ἕν	πλῆθος	φῶς	σκότος
δεξιόν	ἀριστερόν	ἀγαθόν	κακόν
ἄρρεν	θῆλυ	τετράγωνον	ἑτερόμηκες

Heraclitus regarded the existence of such opposites, continually passing the one into the other as necessary to the ἁρμονία of the universe. He taught that we are, and are not; waking is sleeping, day night. But such a shifting nature of phenomena, which this πάντα ῥεῖ theory involves, makes it impossible to predicate anything about them. Heraclitus said that a man could not step twice into the same river; it is a different river by the time he makes his second step; but, according to his own theories, he might have made a more startling statement than this, as Cratylus subsequently pointed out. We can't even step once into a river, for by the time I put foot into the water I am a different man from what I was a yard away from the bank. In fact we can't either say or do anything; how can one affirm that A killed B if everything is changing so quickly that A is a different man before and after the murder? Cratylus saw these difficulties so clearly that he finally refrained from speech and contented himself with pointing his finger!

Parmenides is at the opposite pole from this. According to him the universe is a unity—What is, is—but more than this we cannot say; for to say that something has a quality (e.g. that Socrates is tall) is to say that it is something else, and so its unity is gone at once. If the senses show us certain things which are inconsistent with unity, so much the worse for the senses. What is, is; and anything else is not. But what "is not" cannot be thought; you cannot think of nothing; only that can be, which can be thought. Popular suppositions about things involve the existence of what is not; and so the philosophy of Parmenides denies reality to the negative members, as it were, of the Pythagorean pairs. In any physical sense it is hard to attach much value to these speculations, but they have a most important bearing upon the theory of predication. They make it absolutely essential for philosophy to settle once for all what is designated by the copula *is*. Does it denote existence at all? If I say that Homer is a great poet, does that imply that he is living now? Or again, does it denote identity between the terms related by it? If I say that a cow is a four-footed beast, does that imply that every four-footed beast is a cow? Obviously not; the verb *to be* has some other meaning which has not yet been settled. This theory of predication forms an important part of logic, and the speculations of Parmenides helped it on a stage farther from the impossible flux of Heraclitus. Parmenides restores unity and stability to the world, but it is a unity without content. Because it had not yet been decided what we mean by *is* he thought that we could only say "What is. is " (τὸ ὄν ἐστίν). His argument seems to have been that the world is both a plenum and a unity; that it is a plenum excludes the possibility of motion (for there is no space for things to move into); that it is a unity precludes the possibility of predication, for the idea of a unity amid multiplicity has not yet been conceived. He thus shows us the thorough-going logical outcome of corporeal monism; and his exposition of it ought to have killed it for ever. Had it not been for Parmenides, we might have gone on for ever with rarefaction and condensation theories. Motion is impossible if we confine ourselves to matter; but to make any philosophical advance out of this dead-lock, into which we have landed ourselves, motion must somehow be re-introduced. We have reached a dividing point of philosophy, which henceforward cannot at once be monistic and corporealistic. So far we have been looking at things in their material aspect (ἐν ὕλης εἴδει), but now we see that unity does not belong to that aspect.

2. Zeno

Zeno is well known for a series of remarkable riddles.[1] The most famous is that of Achilles and the tortoise, to the effect that, however little start the tortoise has in a race between the two, Achilles will never be able to overtake it. For before Achilles catches up the tortoise he must first reach the point which the tortoise has just left, and so on *ad infinitum*; the tortoise will always be just a little bit ahead.

In the philosophy of Parmenides the point that struck the popular mind as most paradoxical was the denial of motion, and Zeno determined to support his master's theories by devoting himself to showing that this denial involves less difficulty than does the idea of the existence of motion.

[1] See four of them in Aristotle, "Physica," Z. 9, 239b, 9.

This is the object of all the riddles; and the hearer is expected to conclude, from the absurdities involved, that the appearance of motion is illusion, and that there really can be no such thing.[1]

The indirect support of Eleatic monism which this entails was the sole object of Zeno—an object which Plato in the "Parmenides" represents him as stating very clearly:—

"I see, Parmenides," said Socrates, "that Zeno would not only attach himself to you in general friendship, but also with the support of his writings, for, in a way, they maintain the same position as you do. But he tries to take us in by putting things in a different way, as though his message was different. For you in your poems say that the universe is One, and of this you give excellent and splendid proofs. He, for his part, says that there is no Many, and in support of it gives much weighty evidence. For the one of you thus to affirm the One, and the other to deny the Many, in such a way that, although your doctrines are almost identical, you don't seem to be saying the same thing at all, is a use of language quite beyond the rest of us."

"Yes, Socrates," said Zeno, "but you have not quite grasped the truth about my writings, although you are as good as a Spartan hound in following and tracking down the argument. For you forget that the treatise had no such lofty object as you impute to it, deceiving men as though it were a bigger thing than in reality it was. What you mentioned is an accident, but *in point of fact these writings are intended to support Parmenides' contention against scoffers, who object that many ridiculous and inconsistent results follow upon the affirmation of the One. My treatise is a retort upon those who affirm the existence of the Many*, and it gives them as shrewd and better blows than they inflict,

---

[1] As a matter of fact the absurdities arise from the false conception of space, as something infinitely divisible into a series of discrete points (probably Pythagorean in origin) and of time, as an infinite series of discrete "nows." But time is a *continuum* and so is space; neither can be divided into an infinite number of discrete points or "nows."*
Aristotle saw this, and says that the difficulty "arises from conceiving of time as composed of 'nows,' for if this is not granted the proof will not hold good."

* They are really, as Kant says, Forms of the Sensibility.

THE EARLIER PRE-SOCRATICS

for it shows that upon their hypothesis—the existence of the Many—still more ridiculous results follow than from the existence of the One, if it be only examined adequately" ("Parmenides," 128a).

The italicized sentence, though it refers to the writings of Zeno—and not to the riddles (which he is likely to have used to refute a recalcitrant adversary in conversation)—yet undoubtedly applies to them, and gives us the clue needed to determine his object in busying himself with what, at first sight, appears such childish quibbling.

(c) THE DISCREPANCY BETWEEN ELEATICISM AND PHENOMENA

1. EMPEDOCLES OF ACRAGAS (*circa* 450 B.C.)

Matthew Arnold's poem "Empedocles on Etna" has made this name familiar to all students of English literature; the dramatic end of his life—he committed suicide by leaping into the crater of Etna—gained him a certain notoriety, and throughout his life he seems to have been a somewhat striking figure. Lucretius, who was a discerning man, expresses great admiration for him. In speaking of Sicily, he says, just after mentioning the marvels of Scylla and Charybdis, that there is nothing in the whole of Sicily so fine as Empedocles.[1]

His philosophical system is an attempt to mediate between Eleaticism and the senses. In opposition to the πάντα ῥεῖ of Heraclitus we have seen Parmenides insisting upon unity and stability; τὸ ὄν ἐστίν, change and motion are unreal; the evidence of our senses is illusory.

But this facile contempt of sense-perception would not do for Empedocles. He was in fact much interested in it, and

[1] I. 726.

evolved a theory of sensation—according to which we perceive "like by like," i.e. by means of minute particles (ἀπόρροιαι) or effluences, which flow off from things and impinge upon a similar property in the constitution of the human eye—which is no mean forerunner of Berkeley's theory of vision. We have, in fact, no road to knowledge except through the senses.[1] His conclusion is that what the senses tell us is true in a way; particular things come into being and pass away; but if we look at their ultimate elements or roots (ῥιζώματα) we may say with Parmenides that what is, is—uncreated and indestructible. These ῥιζώματα are four in number—earth, air, fire, and water—and each of them is real in the Parmenidean sense. This is the beginning of the idea of a reality, which is neither created nor destroyed, underlying the shifting nature of phenomena. Another important point in the system of Empedocles is that of the two principles of Love (φιλία) and Strife (νεῖκος) which he posited as alternately predominating. In the combination and dissolution of the ῥιζώματα, we have, not perhaps a very scientific explanation, but at any rate an opening which admits of the possibility of motion, so precipitately banished from philosophy by the Eleatic monists. In the extant fragments of Empedocles there are some interesting lines which show that he had considered the evolution of the animal kingdom. We find a monstrous generation of parts of animals, which only gradually coalesce, and then not

---

[1] In speaking of the nature of the gods, which is not visible, Empedocles remarks that they don't come within our usual means of knowledge :

οὐκ ἔστι πελάσασθαι, οὐδ' ὀφθαλμοῖσιν ἐφικτὸν
ἡμετέροις ἢ χερσὶ λαβεῖν, ᾗπερ γε μεγίστη
πειθοῦς ἀνθρώποισιν ἀμαξιτὸς εἰς φρένα πίπτει.

These lines are imitated by Lucretius, Bk. V. 101 ff.

always in accordance with the anatomical principles of the present day! We read, for example, that on the earth

> Many heads sprung up without necks and arms wandered bare and bereft of shoulders. Eyes strayed up and down in want of foreheads. Many creatures with faces and breasts looking in different directions were born; some, offspring of oxen with faces of men, while others, again, arose as offspring of men with the heads of oxen, and creatures in whom the nature of women and men was mingled, furnished with sterile parts.[1]

2. ANAXAGORAS OF CLAZOMENÆ (500-428 B.C.)

For thirty years of his life (462-432) Anaxagoras lived at Athens, and he was the first great philosopher to do so. Probably he had been brought there by Pericles in pursuance of his dominating idea of Ionizing the Athenians, and he must have exercised a wide influence over the cultured classes of the Periclean age. Euripides, among others, came under his influence, and probably owed to him that rationalizing tendency which is so prominent in his plays. In Plato's "Apology" Socrates says that anyone can hear the views of Anaxagoras for a drachma, i.e. by paying for a seat in the theatre and so hearing his views expounded in the tragedies of Euripides and others. Like Socrates, Anaxagoras was accused on religious grounds for not practising the State religion, and for teaching new ideas about the heavenly bodies (τὰ μετάρσια), e.g. that the sun is a red-hot stone and that the moon is made of earth. But, unlike Socrates, he had a powerful friend and was saved by the intervention of Pericles. Yet the similarity of the case with that of Socrates is most striking; so much so that Socrates in his defence exclaims

---

[1] The translation is taken from Burnet's "Early Greek Philosophy."

that to listen to Meletus one would think that it was Anaxagoras whom he was accusing.[1]

There is some difficulty in constructing a consistent philosophical system out of the fragments of Anaxagoras which have survived. It is highly probable that he was not very consistent himself; at any rate so much is mere matter of interpretation that it seems best to limit ourselves to the attempt to indicate the general lines upon which he attempted to solve the problems that faced him. Like Empedocles, he tried to reconcile the Eleatic doctrine that corporeal substance is unchangeable with the appearance of change with which our senses present us. The conclusions of Parmenides are accepted; nothing can be added to the all, for there cannot be more than all, and the all is always equal to the all (compare the scientific precept of *ex nihilo nihil fit*); but what men call *coming into being* and *passing away* is really *mixture* and *separation* of the component parts of things.

"The Greeks are wrong," he says, "in thinking of the origin and destruction of things, for nothing comes into being and nothing is destroyed, but is mixed and unmixed out of pre-existing things. And they would be more correct in calling 'coming into being' composition and 'destruction' de-composition."

But Anaxagoras did not, like Empedocles, make a distinct separation of the four elements. He says that things are not cut off from one another as by a hatchet, but that there is a portion of everything in everything. What we call the creation of the world is the "unmixing out" of things from Chaos. Specific things are derived from an original medley which consists of σπέρματα τῶν χρημάτων (the seeds of things), each of which though infinitely small contains within itself

[1] Plato, "Apology," 26d (see below, p. 57).

THE EARLIER PRE-SOCRATICS

particles of specific quality, e.g. gold, flesh, bone.[1] In this respect his speculations approximate closely to those of the Atomists, of whom we have next to speak. But he differs from them both in his conception of the σπέρματα themselves, and also—a far more important point—in his conception of the force or principle which causes them συμμίσγεσθαι and διακρίνεσθαι. This is the old difficulty of how to introduce movement into the world. The Atomists proper ascribe it to purely material causes, and it is because he introduced another principle, which he called Intelligence (νοῦς), that Anaxagoras cannot be regarded as an Atomist. Empedocles had ascribed motion to the working of the two principles of νεῖκος and φιλία; Anaxagoras assumes only one. According to him, in the early days of the world everything was mixed together and order was made out of confusion by the action of νοῦς: παντὰ χρήματα, he says, ἦν ὁμοῦ, εἶτα ὁ νοῦς ἐλθὼν αὐτὰ διεκόσμησε. This looks very promising; surely here at last is that action of Intelligence which has been so conspicuous by its absence in all the materialistic theories which we have so far considered. But the hope is false; νοῦς does for Anaxagoras no more than what Love and Strife did for Empedocles. In fact, in some sense, it does less; for its action is only intermittent. It sets things in motion, it is true, and the motion gradually extends and produces two great masses, called Ether and Air. Ether, which is rare, hot, light, and dry, forms the outside of the universe; while Air, which is dense, cold, heavy, and damp, congregates towards the centre. Then νοῦς only enters again, like a *deus ex machina*, when a difficulty arises which cannot be solved by other means.

[1] These portions are often called ὁμοιομερῆ, but the word is Aristotelian and does not belong to Anaxagoras himself who speaks only of σπέρματα.

We have the explicit testimony of Aristotle for this criticism. In the "Metaphysics" he says:—

"Anaxagoras uses his νοῦς as a device for the generation of the universe, and he drags it in whenever he is at a loss to provide a reason for its necessity, but in all other respects he attributes the causation of what is created to anything rather than to νοῦς."

Plato also mentions the disappointment of Socrates when he found what little use Anaxagoras made of the principle of νοῦς.[1] But we must not be too exacting; Anaxagoras marks a distinct advance upon the speculations of previous thinkers, and Aristotle himself admits that contrasted with his predecessors he was like a sober man among madmen.[2]

(d) THE NECESSITY FOR A THEORY OF KNOWLEDGE

1. ATOMISM

Leucippus and Democritus of Abdera are coupled together in our authorities as the great exponents of the atomic theory; except that Leucippus was prior to Democritus we know next to nothing about him; he did exist; but so far as our knowledge of him (apart from Democritus) goes, he might have stood in the same relation to Democritus as Mrs. Harris did to Mrs. Gamp. But he was the founder of the theory of atoms, which may be thus described:[3] "In order to avoid the difficulties connected with the supposition of primitive matter with definite qualities, without admitting the coming into existence and annihilation as realities, and without giving up, as the Eleatic philosophers did, the reality of variety and its changes, the atomists derived all definiteness of phenomena,

---

[1] "Phædo," 98b ff.
[2] "Metaphysics," A. 3, 984b, 18.
[3] The quotation is from the article on "Democritus" in Smith's "Dictionary of Greek and Roman Biography and Mythology" (1844).

both physical and mental, from elementary particles, the infinite number of which were homogeneous in quality, but heterogeneous in form." The development of the theory will be familiar to the classical student from his reading of Lucretius, and its natural origin from the ὁμοιομερῆ of Anaxagoras ought not to escape the reader of this book. But what has all this got to do with a theory of knowledge? The answer lies in the nature of the explanation of reality which it involves. The original question of Thales, as to what is the nature of Being, or of the existing universe, has now been answered in a manner which takes reality to be something very different from what our senses present to us. Consequently, there is a marked tendency in the period of philosophical speculation at which we are now arrived, to overstep the limits of Cosmology and to take up subjects which belong to a theory of cognition. What we may call the Theory of Being has defined reality in terms so contrary to the evidence of our eyes, that it is bound to present us with some theory of perception. This we have already seen in the ἀπόρροιαι of Empedocles; next, this theory of perception naturally leads to a theory of knowledge. If the atoms are ultimate reality (and they are different enough from the phenomena known to our senses!), then we must give some account of the difference between appearance and reality. All this is not explicitly recognized in the philosophers of the period; but it is implied by the distinction which Democritus made between true and false knowledge (γνησίη and σκοτίη γνῶσις), and between what really (ἐτεῇ) is and what is only commonly supposed to be (νόμῳ). He says that hot and cold, sweet and bitter are commonly supposed to be, but that really there is nothing but void and the atoms.

2. Democritus as an Ethical Philosopher

We cannot separate Democritus from Leucippus so far as his atomism is concerned; but in many respects he is obviously a precursor of Socrates, of whom he was, so far as dates go, a contemporary. He certainly belonged to the age after Protagoras (of whom we have still to treat), but owing to his connexion with Leucippus it is convenient to consider him here. He was born at Abdera about the year 460 B.C., and the date of his death is given in various years between 370 and 357. He came of a wealthy family, and spent much of his time in travelling about the world studying men and cities. Perhaps he had something of the urbanity of the cosmopolitan with its large tolerance for the follies of men —a trait which may have given rise to his nickname of "the laughing philosopher," just as Heraclitus was called "the weeping philosopher."[1]

Diogenes Laertius tells us that in his ethical philosophy Democritus regarded the *summum bonum* of life as peace of mind (εὐθυμία); such peace of mind and freedom from fear is one of the chief products of the study of philosophy.[2] That his teaching was of a high order is obvious from his remark that there is no virtue in the abstaining from wrongdoing unless there is also the absence of the wish to do wrong— ἀγαθὸν οὐ τὸ μὴ ἀδικεῖν, ἀλλὰ τὸ μηδὲ ἐθέλειν. He had some idea, too, of the universality of the moral qualities; all men, he says, respect goodness and truth—ἀνθρώποισι πᾶσι σέβαστά ἐστι τὸ ἀγαθὸν καὶ ἀληθές·ἡδὺ δὲ ἄλλο ἄλλῳ. These are ideas which we shall find frequent in Socrates and Plato.

---

[1] Cf. Juvenal, X. 28 ff.
[2] Cf. the avowed object of Lucretius in writing his *De rerum natura*.

CHAPTER III

THE SOPHISTS

ACCORDING to the derivation of the word, the sophists were simply wise men; but they belong to a definite period of Greek culture, and the word came to be used—largely as the result of Plato's polemic against them—in a peculiar and derogatory sense. To-day the word is almost a synonym of " quibbler," and we shall see how such a specialization of meaning has set in. But first of all the use of the word implied no such reproach (Socrates is a sophist in this sense), and it was only gradually, along with the rise of a definitely professional class of teachers who taught for pay, i.e. made a living out of their profession, that the word came to have any such connotation. These sophists were partly the cause and partly the result of the new social and intellectual conditions which obtained at Athens in the period which we may call the period of the New Culture—roughly speaking from about 450 to 400 B.C. They were originally not themselves Athenians by birth, but flocked to Athens from all parts of the Greek world, attracted thither by the growing demand for higher education, and by the scope which Athenian political life gave to the art of rhetoric. In considering this new culture we must remember two things: (1) that general conversation and definite oral teaching supplied the place of newspapers and books in our own time; (2) that every educated Athenian took a personal part

The New Culture.

in the government of his city (either as a special magistrate, member of the Boule or of the Ecclesia). These two facts occasioned a general and a particular demand; both of which were supplied by the sophists. By settling at Athens and gathering the young men of the day around them they made themselves responsible for the equivalent of a modern university education; and, in particular, they professed to teach the art of citizenship. When so much political business both in the Boule and in the Ecclesia was conducted by means of speeches, it is not surprising to find tremendous importance attached to the art of rhetoric; skill in speaking would be essential to "getting on in life," for in a lawsuit, for example —and the Athenians were very litigious—a skilful pleader would have a very practical advantage over his less skilful adversary; he would be able to put his case in the best possible light. This is what is meant by τὸν ἥττω λόγον κρείττω ποιεῖν, not in itself an immoral procedure. But, when it is made the definite aim of instruction, we can readily understand how the ideals first of the pupil, and then of the teacher, become quite estranged from any consideration of the truth, or the pursuit of knowledge for its own sake. And so the aim of sophistical training becomes the rhetorical persuasion of one's fellow-men[1] rather than the disinterested elucidation of truth. From this it is but a short step to "sophistry" in the most derogatory sense of the word. But we must not allow such a connotation to enter into our ideas of the first great sophists such as

1. Protagoras of Abdera

Though born, like Democritus, at Abdera, Protagoras by no means spent his life there; like other sophists he travelled

[1] Plato, "Gorgias," 453a, πειθοῦς δημιουργός ἐστιν ἡ ῥητορική.

THE SOPHISTS

about the world settling now in this centre and now in that, and giving a course of lectures to all who chose to come—and pay. He would probably be accompanied from place to place by the more intimate of his pupils. One of the best-attested facts of his life is that he framed a code of laws for the Athenian Colony of Thurii in S. Italy which was founded in 444-3 B.C. He made two visits to Athens, of the second of which we have a vivid record in Plato's dialogue called after him, and this cannot well have taken place after the outbreak of the Peloponnesian war in 432 B.C. We may take it, then, that his life filled the greater part of the fifth century.

In Plato's dialogue we find Protagoras professing to train young men as virtuous citizens; he is made to say:—

"If Hippocrates comes to me he will not experience what he would if he went to any other sophist. For the rest of them treat young men shamefully—when they have just escaped from the arts they lead them back again against their will and force them to resume calculation and astronomy and geometry and music (here he glanced at Hippias), whereas if he comes to me he will simply learn what he came for. And this is prudence, both concerning the private and the public affairs of life, how to manage his own household to the best advantage, and how to make himself most efficient both in word and deed in directing the affairs of the State." "Do I understand you?" said I. "I think you speak of political science, and undertake to make men good citizens." "That is just the undertaking," said he, "which I do make, Socrates."[1]

This at once raises the question as to whether virtue can be taught or not. Socrates confesses himself very sceptical upon the point; but the question belongs to Socratic philosophy and must not be treated here.

In the teaching of Protagoras himself the most outstanding feature was its subjectivity: there can be no ultimate right and wrong; things are what they seem to me to be; πάντων μέτρον ἄνθρωπος.

[1] Plato, "Protagoras," 318d.

man is the measure of all things—πάντων χρημάτων μέτρον ἄνθρωπος.

2. Gorgias of Leontini

Gorgias belongs to the same generation as Protagoras; he came as an ambassador from Leontini to Athens in 427 B.C. (much as Mr. Balfour in 1917 went to America) to obtain help for the Ionic Sicilians against the Dorians. He was perhaps more of a rhetorician than of a philosopher; but we have a triad of arguments said to have been maintained by him. They are, firstly, that nothing exists; secondly, that if anything existed it could not be apprehended by us; and, thirdly, that if these first two things were possible, yet our thought could not be expressed in language and communicated to others. At first sight this looks very much like the sophistry which we have said was not typical of the earlier sophists; but it only needs understanding to show that this is not so.

<small>His Three Theses.</small>

1. "That nothing exists" is simply due to the confusion between the existential and the propositional use of *is*. From the statement "Gorgias is an ambassador from Leontini," I am not likely to acquire any doubts about *is* denoting existence, but I am from the statement that "A griffin is a fire-breathing dragon," if I have any scepticism in me at all.

2. The contention that if anything existed it could not be apprehended is similarly due to the total opposition between the subjective and the objective side of things, which had till now been a distinctive mark of all philosophical thinking. I can think of the non-existent quite as readily as of the existent. Thought is therefore no criterion of existence, for there is an unbridgeable gulf—or at least a gulf which philosophy

THE SOPHISTS

has not yet bridged—between me and the external universe or *non-ego*.

3. The third contention of Gorgias seems to rest upon the feeling of the impossibility of identifying where there is a difference;[1] a word cannot *be* a visual object, so it seems difficult to imagine how words can give an adequate representation to a second person of my perceptions.

But without going into details we see a sufficient explanation of these three contentions in the relation in which Gorgias stood to Eleaticism, and in particular to Zeno. As the reader has seen, Zeno attempted to support Parmenides by stressing the inconsistencies involved in the conceptions of multiplicity and motion; Gorgias seizes upon the same arguments, and concludes that, since existence involves such contradictions, therefore nothing exists!

But what is the use of such metaphysical speculations? ῥητορική. As Grote says,[2] "It may fairly be presumed that these doctrines were urged by Gorgias for the purpose of diverting his disciples from studies which he considered as unpromising and fruitless." And thus we see him in Plato's dialogue, which bears his name, maintaining the superiority of ῥητορική to all such vain speculations. To the question of Socrates as to what is the greatest good of man, and of which he says that he is the creator, he replies:—

What is really, Socrates, the greatest good, and the cause alike of freedom for individuals themselves and of rule over others in their respective cities.

Socrates. What do you say that this is?

---

[1] We have already mentioned (see above, p. 35) that the idea of a unity amid multiplicity is a conception at which philosophy has not yet arrived. The lack of such a concep ion explains the whole signi ficance of Eleaticism in its logical aspect.

[2] "History of Greece," Vol. VI. p. 71 (1862 ed.).

Gorgias. I should say the ability to persuade by one's speeches judges in the law-courts, counsellors in the council-chamber, and citizens in the assembly, or in whatsoever other political meeting may be held. By means of this power you will make the physician your slave and the trainer your slave; and the business man of ours will turn out to be making money, not for himself, but for another—for you, who are able to make a speech and persuade the crowd.[1]

3. Thrasymachus of Chalcedon

Thrasymachus was a contemporary of Gorgias, and is known to us as an interlocutor in Plato's "Republic," where he quite justifies his name as a bold, or even rash, fighter.[2] He is mentioned in the earliest comedy of Aristophanes ("The Banqueters," of which only fragments are extant), which was produced in 427 B.C.—the year of Plato's birth and that in which Gorgias came to Athens. Plato is not likely to have attributed to him doctrines inconsistent with his actual teaching—for as Thrasymachus was only one generation removed from Plato the fraud would have been at once denounced—so we may take the words put into his mouth in the "Republic" as substantially correct. He there maintains the doctrine that Might is Right; there is no such thing as abstract justice; it is merely the interest of the stronger (τὸ τοῦ κρείττονος συμφέρον) which enables him to impose his will upon the weaker. This is subjected to a searching examination by the dialectic of Socrates until Thrasymachus finally loses his temper and takes refuge in vulgar abuse. But the statement is interesting to us here, as involving a denial of any ultimate standard in morality; it is part and parcel of the whole subjectivism of the sophistic movement.

[1] Plato, "Gorgias," 452d. [2] See below, p. 77.

4. EUTHYDEMUS OF CHIOS

Euthydemus lived for some time with his brother Dionysodorus at Thurii in Italy; they were both banished from there and came to live at Athens. They figure prominently in Plato's dialogue "Euthydemus" as mighty "throwers" who can refute any argument by whomsoever advanced, and no matter how true or false it may be. They represent the "eristic" side of the sophistic movement, which with its sophisms and quibbles reminds us of nothing so much as of the Eleatic riddles of Zeno. They also, like Protagoras and Gorgias, profess to teach virtue and believe that they can do so better and more quickly than any other man. They are induced by Socrates to give an exhibition of their art and as a result are involved in a series of dialectical tangles and pitfalls which make the "Euthydemus" the most amusing of Plato's dialogues.

5. THE PHILOSOPHICAL SIGNIFICANCE OF THE SOPHISTS

Subjectivity.

The philosophical significance of the sophistic movement is that it stresses the "subjective" side of things. It is realized that knowledge is more than mere passive perception; external things are not, as it were, *given* "de facto," as such, leaving us nothing to do but to take in the impressions. The relation between the known object and the knowing person is not one-sided; there is an element contributed by the "knower." This is very obvious in the case of sense-perception—take colours, for example; they are not isolated qualities of things, existing in and by themselves apart from all percipient subjects, but relations between the sun, as the source of light, the surface of the particular body and the human eye. This will be painfully obvious to me if the "subjective" factor in my case is distorted, i.e. if something goes wrong with my eyes. And so with knowledge; it is a hopeless quest to ask about *things-in-themselves;* for, if we did ever succeed in getting to know anything about them, they would *ipso facto* become *things-in-relation-to-us*. This is what is meant by "the relativity of knowledge," and means no more than that, the human mind being constituted as it is, things can be apprehended by it only under certain aspects, as it were, or in certain forms—in space and time for example. Try to think of something outside of space, or beyond time, and you will see what is meant. Now the sophists seized upon this essential relation of things to man, and unduly stressed the subjective side. From the truth that things *are* what they appear to man (in the sense of *mankind*, οἱ ἄνθρωποι) they falsely concluded that they are what they appear to each individual man; for such seems to have been the meaning attached by Protagoras to his πάντων χρημάτων μέτρον ἄνθρωπος. This has important results as regards—

1. Epistemology, or the theory of knowledge.
2. Ethics, or the theory of conduct.

Such extreme subjectivism is as disastrous, in our desire to build up a system of knowledge, as was the supposed perpetual flux of things in the objective world according to the theories of Heraclitus. Neither Protagoras nor Gorgias can give me any criterion of truth; both are equally subjective; the only difference is that, according to the one, whatever man thinks is true; while according to the other, whatever man thinks is false! It is the same in the sphere of ethics; extreme subjectivism does away with the distinction between right and wrong. There can be no absolute right and wrong; men merely consider certain actions right and others wrong, and what is wrong with one set of people may be right with another. In fact, it is all a matter of convention (νόμῳ) and there is no such natural difference (φύσει) between the two classes of acts which we respectively call right and wrong.

This is the ethical doctrine which we shall find attacked by Socrates, the world's greatest moral teacher; but we must admit that it does contain an element of truth, which has been very much stressed by modern ethical writers with an anthropological turn of mind. They have been influenced by the reports of anthropologists as to the very divergent ideas about right and wrong among the different races of mankind. But such writers, as is usually the case, tend to imagine that their discoveries—which are true in certain cases—must necessarily be true in all cases; whereas the truth of the matter is that all actions, which are usually regarded as moral actions (πράξεις), are not of one type. They are, in fact, of at least two[1] distinct kinds—there are those which are only conventionally (νόμῳ) right and wrong (e.g. monogamy among Christians, and polygamy among Mohammedans), and it is to these alone that the "anthropological" arguments apply; and there are those which are absolutely (φύσει) right and wrong according to the eternal, unwritten, laws of humanity, to which Antigone appeals in the noble lines of Sophocles.[2]

[1] We leave out of account actions which are right or wrong only in virtue of some human ordinance or Act of Parliament, as it were. Such actions have no peculiar moral sanction of their own (whether conventional or absolute) and their connexion with morality resides only in the *obedience* to law, as such, which is part of the duty of every good citizen.

[2] "Antigone," 450 ff.

CHAPTER IV

SOCRATES AND A THEORY OF CONDUCT

AFTER the age of the Sophists, with all its subjectivity, it is not surprising to find that the interest of philosophy has shifted from the objective world to the microcosm of man. Just as the purely physical or cosmological speculations of philosophy, from the crude suppositions of Thales to the matured atomism of Democritus, led inevitably from a Theory of Being to a Theory of Knowledge, so the subjective nature of that theory of knowledge—as presented by the Sophists —with all its stress upon the individual, inevitably centres the whole interest of philosophy in man himself. The social conditions of the time—the close connexion between rhetoric and political power, and the great importance of speech in the higher education of the day—all tended in the same direction. From the very conditions of his age, then, Socrates (470-399 B.C.) was bound to have a great interest in ethics. This interest was not, however, predominant with him at first; in his youth he was much interested in the cosmological speculations of the earlier philosophy, and this explains one of the two great mysteries connected with him.

The "Clouds" of Aristophanes. The two mysteries are (1) the attack which is made upon him in the " Clouds " of Aristophanes, and (2) his condemnation at the hands of the Athenians for impiety. Now the " Clouds " was produced in 423 B.C.; it cannot therefore refer to any-

thing in the last twenty-five years in the life of Socrates—
the quarter of a century of his maturity—and the philosopher
whom Aristophanes caricatures so ludicrously " walking the
air,"[1] and studying τὰ μετέωρα from a basket slung in mid-
air, is the young Socrates whom we know to have been a
student of the cosmological theories of Anaxagoras and
others. The second mystery (the condemnation for impiety)
is even more puzzling; how did such a great moral teacher
as Socrates, a man who led a blameless personal life, and in
his teaching held up the highest ideals of conduct to others,
come himself to be condemned to death, and that for impiety
of all things? The charge was one of "corrupting the
youth" and "recognizing strange gods," and we cannot
understand it at all unless we bear in mind two things : (1)
that in the πόλις or city-state the man who took no part in
politics was regarded with extreme suspicion ; (2) that religion in such a small community as that of the πόλις is much
more a matter of *cultus*—of definite religious observances,
sanctioned and directed by the State—than it is with us to-
day. Now we know that Socrates abstained from political
life (his δαιμόνιον, for which see below, he himself tells us,
forbade his participation), and contented himself with conversing on all occasions and in all places with such as chose
to attach themselves to him as disciples. In the "Apology"
of Plato (23a) Socrates is made to describe how these young
men loved to come around him and listen to his examination
of would-be wiseacres, and how they themselves would
imitate him and expose the ignorance of people who were
reputed to be wise. Plato represents this as a contributory
cause of the odium into which he would have us believe that

The Condemnation for Impiety.

[1] ἀεροβατῶ καὶ περιφρονῶ τὸν ἥλιον. Aristoph., "Clouds," 225.

Socrates had fallen with his fellow-men; but it more probably contains only a half-truth, the whole of which we can fill out for ourselves when we remember that the disciples of Socrates included such men as Critias and Alcibiades. For what is more likely than that the Athenians should have come to regard Socrates as the head of an anti-democratic *clique*, who purposely abstained himself from all participation in the affairs of his city—in itself, according to Greek ideas, a sufficiently suspicious circumstance—in order to work the more effectively as a "power behind the scenes" through the medium of his disciples?[1] When we realize the conditions of the age, the idea seems by no means unreasonable— no more unreasonable, at least, than that even "good" Roman Emperors should have persecuted the Christians under the impression that people who held secret clandestine meetings must be political malcontents plotting to overturn the newly-established Empire. Then, as to the second point, Professor A. E. Taylor has shown[2] that "the Platonic 'Apology' vindicates Socrates triumphantly on the score of 'atheism,' but silently owns that he was guilty on the real charge of unlicensed innovation in religion." Socrates was on friendly terms with many of the Pythagoreans of his time, and was certainly a devout believer in many Pythagorean doctrines

---

[1] It used to be assumed that the accusation was a "trumped up" charge, an act of political revenge for Socrates' action in the debate about the condemnation of the generals who failed to pick up the dead and wounded after the battle of Arginusæ, which brought him into disfavour with the *demos*, and for his disobedience of the Thirty (see "Apology," 32), which brought upon him odium with the oligarchic party; but A. E. Taylor has shown in his "Varia Socratica" (First Series) that this cannot be the true explanation. I am much indebted to his paper in what I have suggested above.

[2] In "Varia Socratica" (*supra*).

SOCRATES AND A THEORY OF CONDUCT 57

(e.g. life after death). It is not so much that these doctrines were themselves discredited, as that those who held them— the Pythagoreans—were regarded with suspicion. They were "foreigners;" many of them too had played an anti-democratic part in the political troubles at Croton, which led to the break-up of the Pythagorean brotherhood in Magna Græcia. Anyone, then, who embraced doctrines which were obviously Pythagorean in origin would easily be involved in the odium in which the Pythagoreans were undoubtedly held by the Athenian democracy. Their political action was, not unnaturally, regarded as intimately bound up with their religious beliefs; and so, startling as the condemnation of Socrates for impiety does at first sight appear, there is really no reason to convict either Anytus or Meletus of insincerity or of any bad motive in the charge which they brought against him.

In considering Socrates as a philosopher it would be impossible to attach too much importance to his personality as a man. When we think of him conversing daily in the market-place upon topics of every description, but always bringing the conversation round to some great moral issue, such as "What is virtue?" or "What is justice?" and always with his habitual εἰρωνεία disclaiming knowledge himself, but attempting to elicit the opinions of others, we cannot doubt that we have here to deal with one of the strongest personalities in the history of the world. Snub-nosed himself and by no means well featured—if not positively ugly—he yet fascinated the ἔφηβοι of his day and, among them, the handsome and careless Alcibiades. A particular mark of his strong personality is to be found in that "heavenly sign"— τὸ δαιμόνιον—of which he himself makes frequent mention. Voice of conscience, intuition, or whatever it may have been,

His Personality.

τὸ δαιμόνιον.

it is certainly the sign of a unique personality. He tells us that he has had it from childhood, and that it is an inward monitor which warns him whenever he is about to do anything wrong.[1] (It should be noted that it is always deterrent in its promptings, and never impels to action.) And, surely, it was no ordinary man who neglected the usual affairs of life—to such an extent that even by the end of his life he had no possessions—in order that he might devote himself to instigating his fellow-men to a more whole-hearted pursuit of virtue. Well might he tell his judges that, if they killed him, they would not find another like him to act as a sort of "gadfly" sent by heaven to stir into life the great and noble but sluggish "steed" of Athens.[2] It may readily be believed that the personality of such a man must count for even more than his actual doctrine.

The Historical and the Platonic Socrates.
When we come to consider his doctrine, we have first to distinguish between the *historical* Socrates and the *dramatis persona* of that name in the dialogues of Plato. Of recent years [3] we have come to regard much more of what we read about Socrates in the pages of Plato as being truly representative of Socratic doctrine than we formerly did. In short, we perceive that Plato the disciple has *interpreted* the teachings of his great master Socrates, and not used his name as a convenient peg upon which to hang his own doctrines. Nevertheless, it is unfortunate that Socrates never committed anything to writing, though we can obtain an absolutely certain *minimum* of Socratic doctrine by following the time-honoured plan of comparing our two authorities —Xenophon and Plato—and concluding that that at least is

---

[1] "Apology," 31d. [2] *Ib.*, 30e.
[3] Largely owing to the exegesis of A. E. Taylor and John Burnet.

SOCRATES AND A THEORY OF CONDUCT 59

Socratic which is common to both of them. We have also the definite statement of Aristotle, who assigns two things to the historical Socrates—(1) ἐπακτικοὶ λόγοι, and (2) τὸ ὁρίζεσθαι καθόλου. Ἐπακτικοὶ λόγοι are inductive arguments, ἡ διαλεκ- and are a means to "general definition," by which we obtain, τική. for example, some general definition of justice as a result of examining a number of actions which are considered just. These are two parts of the famous dialectic—ἡ διαλεκτική— of Socrates, of which we will shortly give examples from Plato's dialogues; but we will first quote from Xenophon to prove that this διαλεκτική was really Socratic and not due to Plato. At the beginning of the "Memorabilia" he tells us Socrates was accustomed continually to discuss, with all and sundry, everything that concerned man in both the social and the private affairs of life—all those things of which, if a man is ignorant, he is no better than a slave;[1] and later on he gives us an example as follows:—

And if anyone were to oppose him about a matter without having anything clear to say, but merely urging without proof that he was wiser than the man whom Socrates named, or more skilled in politics, or braver, or anything else of the sort, he would bring back (ἐπανῆγεν) the whole argument to its original assumption in some such manner as this: "You say that the man whom you praise is a better citizen than my man?—I do. Then why not first consider this point, What is the duty of a good citizen?—Let us do so. Well, then, in the management of finance, he would be superior who makes the State better off in money matters?—Certainly. And in war he who assures it victory over its antagonists?—Clearly. And on an embassy would it not be the man who can make friends instead of enemies?—Presumably. And in addressing the people will it not therefore be he who puts an end to factions, and inspires harmony?—I think so." When the arguments were thus brought back to fundamentals (ἐπαναγομένων), the truth would become clear even to those who opposed them. And whenever he himself expounded a matter in argument, he would proceed

[1] Xenophon, "Memorabilia," I. 1, 16.

by means of the most generally admitted truths, considering that safety in argument lay in such a procedure. And so, whenever he conversed, he obtained the agreement of his listeners far more than any other man whom I know. And he said that Homer himself attributed to Odysseus the power of being an irrefutable pleader, in that he was able to conduct his arguments by means of pleas which all men conceded. ("Memorabilia," IV. 6, 13-15).

Such is Xenophon's account of what Aristotle calls ἐπακτικοὶ λόγοι (notice the verbs ἐπανῆγεν and ἐπαναγομένων); let us now see what account he gives of Aristotle's second point (τὸ ὁρίζεσθαι καθόλου) :—

I will also try to show that he made his associates more skilful dialecticians. For Socrates held that those who knew the nature of existing things could expound it to others also, but that in the case of those who did not know it was not to be wondered at that they should both be deceived themselves and deceive others. And so he never ceased to examine, along with his associates, into the nature of existing things. It would be a heavy task to recount all of his definitions; but I will mention such as I consider to show the method of his inquiry. And first concerning piety he would inquire as follows :—

"Tell me, Euthydemus," he said, "what sort of a thing do you think piety is?" And he replied, "A very fine thing, by Heavens." "Can you state what sort of a man the pious man is?" "The man, as I think, who honours the gods," he replied. "Is it allowable to honour the gods in whatsoever fashion a man pleases?" "No, there are laws in accordance with which we must honour them." "So the man who knows these laws would know how he ought to honour the gods, wouldn't he?" "I think so," he said. "Now, surely he who knows how he ought to honour the gods does not imagine that he ought to do so in a manner different from what he knows to be right, does he?" "By no means," he said. "And does a man honour the gods in a manner different from what he thinks he should?" "I think not," he said. "So the man who knows the lawful enactments about the gods would honour the gods in a lawful manner?" "Certainly." "And he who honours them in a lawful manner does so as he should?" "Surely." "And he who honours them as he should is a pious man?" "Certainly," he said. "So we should be right, shouldn't we, in defining the pious man as he who knows the lawful enactments about the gods?" "So I at least think," he replied ("Memorabilia," IV. 6, 1-4).

SOCRATES AND A THEORY OF CONDUCT 61

By such dialectic, which he may have learnt from Zeno, Socrates tries to find the *One* in the *Many*, that unity which is not identity, but a unity amid diversity—a principle the lack of which we have seen causing difficulties in the theory of predication as hitherto understood—which is, perhaps, the greatest contribution of Socrates to the progress of logic, and a great step towards the final epistemology of Plato. The nature of this is clear even from Xenophon's brief account of the attempt to determine the nature of εὐσεβεία ; but we will give a longer example of the fully developed διαλεκτική as shown in one of Plato's dialogues. We will take it from the "Meno," because that dialogue contains many very Socratic things. It is, for example, the best commentary upon his playful comparison[1] between his own art (διαλεκτική) and that of his mother (μαιευτική). Just as his mother helped μαιευτική. others to bring children into the world, so Socrates helps others to bring their thoughts to birth ; for example, he tells Theætetus, at the end of the dialogue which bears his name, that he must not be disappointed at the unsatisfactory nature of the conclusions reached ; he may chance to conceive again, and in any case he will be the better for having got rid of a good many misconceptions. The young slave of Menon would seem to have been a very good subject, for a knowledge of Euclid, I. 47, is evolved from one who had never studied geometry ![2]

At the outset of the dialogue Socrates, who is seeking for Διαλεκ-a definition of ἀρετή—after causing surprise by confessing, τική illus-with his usual εἰρωνεία, that he does not know what it is— trated from is given by his interlocutor nothing but *instances*, as it (a) The "Meno."

---

[1] "Theætetus," 210c.
[2] This is a good illustration of ἀνάμνησις (see below, under Plato, p. 109).

were, nothing but *particular* ἀρεταί, or, as he himself exclaims, σμῆνός τι ἀρετῶν—a whole bee-hive of virtues—whereas he wants to know what virtue itself is, to find that which makes us call all these particular virtues by the name of ἀρετή—the ἓν εἶδος δι' ὃ εἰσὶν ἀρεταί.[1] He wants the general definition, as Aristotle calls it (τὸ ὁρίζεσθαι καθόλου), and he attempts to find it by a series of ἐπακτικοὶ λόγοι as follows :—

M. In my opinion, then, Socrates, virtue, as the poet has it, is " To rejoice in what is fair and to have the power to do so ; " and this is what I think virtue is, to long for what is fair and to be able to gain it. *S.* Do you mean that he who longs for the fair also longs for the good? *M.* Certainly I do. *S.* And when you speak thus do you suppose that some there are who long for what is evil, others for what is fair? You do not believe, my friend, that everybody longs for what is good? *M.* I do not. *S.* Then some long for the evil? *M.* Yes. *S.* Do you mean that they think the evil good, or that they are not ignorant of what is evil but still long for it? *M.* I mean both. *S.* Then do you think, Menon, that there are people who realize that evil is evil, but nevertheless long for it? *M.* Certainly. *S.* What do you mean by "long for"? Do you mean "long to have"? *M.* Yes, to have. What else do you think? *S.* Then do they think that evil benefits him who has it, or do they realize that it injures whomsoever it approaches? *M.* There are some who think that evil benefits them, others who realize that it does them harm. *S.* Do you think that those who imagine that evil benefits them, realize evil to be evil? *M.* I hardly think so. *S.* Then is it not obvious that these men do not long for evil, who are ignorant of what it is, but rather long for things which they imagine to be good, but which are really evil? So that those who are ignorant of this, and think that these things are good, obviously long for what is good. Is it not so? *M.* It seems to be the case. *S.* What follows? Those who long for evil things, as you say, and believe that evil things will harm whomsoever they approach, realize surely that they will themselves receive harm from such things? *M.* Undoubtedly. *S.* Then do they not know that those who receive harm are miserable, in so far as they are harmed? *M.* This too they undoubtedly know.

---

[1] The full significance of this expression will not be apparent until we have considered the Platonic " Ideas " (see below, p. 107).

S. And the miserable are unhappy? *M.* I suppose so. *S.* Then is there anybody who wishes to be miserable and unhappy? *M.* I do not think so. *S.* Then nobody, Menon, wishes for evil things, unless he wishes to be in such a plight. For what else is it to be miserable, if not to long for evil things and to acquire them? *M.* What you say seems to be true, Socrates, and no man wishes for evil. *S.* Now you said just now, did you not, that virtue is "to wish for good things, and to have power over them?" *M.* I said so. *S.* But from what we have just said, all men may wish for good things, so in this respect one man is no better than another? *M.* It seems so. *S.* Then it is obvious that if one man is better than another, it is with respect to having power over them that he would be better. *M.* Certainly. *S.* This, then, according to your definition, is virtue, the power of gaining good things. *M.* Yes, it seems to me to be exactly as you understand it now. *S.* Now let us see if what you say now is true: for you may speak aright. To be able to gain good things you say is virtue? *M.* I do. *S.* And by good things do you not mean such things as health and wealth? *M.* And to gain silver and gold in the city, and honours and offices. *S.* You do not mean anything else, when you speak of good things, than such as these? *M.* No. I mean all such things. *S.* Very well. To gain silver and gold is virtue; so says Menon, the hereditary guest of the great king. But would you not make an addition to this acquisition, Menon, and say to gain justly and piously? Or is it all the same to you, and even if a man gains these things unjustly, you call it virtue none the less? *M.* Certainly not, Socrates, I call it vice. *S.* Then this acquisition, so it seems, must by all means be accompanied by justice, or temperance, or piety, or some other part of virtue; otherwise it will not be virtue, even though it provides good things. *M.* How could it be virtue without? *S.* Then not to gain silver and gold, neither for oneself nor for anybody else, when it would not be just, is not this non-acquisition also virtue? *M.* It seems so. *S.* Then the acquisition of such good things, so it seems, is no more virtue than the non-acquisition, but what is gained with justice is virtue, what is gained without any such thing is vice. *M.* I think it must be as you say. *S.* Now did we not say a moment ago that each of these things is a part of virtue, justice, temperance, and the like? *M.* Yes. *S.* So you are playing with me, Menon? *M.* What do you mean, Socrates? *S.* Because when I begged you not long ago, not to break up virtue and chop it into pieces, and when I gave you examples according to which you should answer, you took no notice of it, but you say now that virtue is "to be able to gain good things with justice," and this you say is a part of virtue. *M.* I do. *S.* Then does it not follow from what you say, that to do whatever one does with a part of virtue, is virtue? For justice you say is but a part of virtue, and so with each of these things. *M.* What then? *S.* I mean this, that, although I begged you to talk of virtue as a whole, you are far from telling me what virtue itself is, but you say that every act is virtue if only it is performed with a part of virtue; as if you had already told me what virtue is as a whole, and as if I understand even though you chop it up into pieces. Now you must start again from the beginning with this question, my dear Menon, "What is virtue?" or should it be said that every act performed with a part of virtue, is virtue? For it is to say this, when one says that every act performed with justice, is virtue. Do you not think we ought to start again with the same question? Do you think a man can know what a part of virtue is, but not know what virtue is itself? *M.* I do not think so ("Meno," 77b-79c, 9).

If we analyse the above argument we find, as so often with Socrates, three definite stages, three successive propositions put forward; or, rather, an original proposition twice amended under stress of διαλεκτική.

1. First, virtue is said to consist in the love and attainment of the honourable (ἐπιθυμοῦντα τῶν καλῶν δυνατὸν εἶναι πορίζεσθαι), and Menon admits that he makes no distinction between ἀγαθά and καλά.

2. Secondly, as all men desire what seems good to them— the objects of some ἐπιθυμίαι are κακά, but they are not desired as κακά—the first half of the definition is a negligible constant, and the rest of it may be more briefly put as δύναμις τοῦ πορίζεσθαι τἀγαθά.

3. But, seeing that things may be acquired both justly and unjustly, we must emend this definition to something like οἷόν τε εἶναι τἀγαθὰ πορίζεσθαι μετὰ δικαιοσύνης (which is itself a *part* of ἀρετή). This is equivalent to attempting to

define the whole in terms of a part, and so we must drop this line of inquiry and make a fresh start.

These same three movements, as it were, of Socratic διαλεκτική may be illustrated from the "Euthydemus," that exciting match against a couple of Sophists which is as good as any comedy. Socrates there begins, as usual, with some commonly accepted statement,[1] such as that all men desire to be happy and prosperous—πάντες ἄνθρωποι βουλόμεθα εὖ πράττειν; then we get as a preliminary definition the proposition that he εὖ πράττει who has many ἀγαθά such as πλοῦτος, ὑγιεία and σοφία. Εὐτυχία is at first included, but is at once ruled out as being included in σοφία, for in any art it is knowledge that brings success. But none of these goods helps a man by its mere existence; he only derives benefit from them if he employs them. So we get, as a beginning of the second movement of the argument, the definition of εὐδαιμονία as τό τε κεκτῆσθαι τἀγαθά καὶ τὸ χρῆσθαι αὐτοῖς. Now, there is a wrong and a right use of everything, and these ἀγαθά are likely to make a man happy only if he uses them correctly (ἐὰν ὀρθῶς χρῆται). So the third stage of the argument results in the conclusion that σοφία is an ἀγαθόν and ἀμαθία a κακόν. Such a conclusion is part of the main principle of Socrates' ethical teaching. He maintained that virtue is knowledge (ἀρετή = ἐπιστήμη). "No man," said he, "is willingly evil" (οὐδεὶς ἑκὼν κακός). We have Xenophon's evidence for this. He states quite explicitly:—

(b) The "Euthydemus."

Virtue is Knowledge.

"He said that justice and every other virtue was wisdom. For just actions and everything done with virtue was honourable and good, and no one who knew these things would ever choose anything else in preference to them, but those who knew them not could not perform them,

---

[1] Cf. Xenophon, "Memorabilia," IV. 6, 15, διὰ τῶν μάλιστα ὁμολογουμένων ἐπορεύετο, quoted above, p. 60.

but even if they tried, would go wrong; and that the wise accordingly did what was honourable and good, but that those who were not wise could not do so, but went wrong even if they tried. Since therefore all just actions, and all actions that are honourable and good, are done with virtue, it is clear that justice and every other virtue is wisdom" ("Memorabilia," III. 9, 5).

This sounds like a very paradoxical doctrine; and it will be objected at once that intellectual achievements have, often enough, nothing to do with moral virtue. But, rightly understood, it contains a great deal of truth; surely there is a moral value in education; no one will maintain that, if a boy has been brought up on "the best that has been thought and said in the world"—to use Matthew Arnold's expression —his reading will have had no ennobling effect upon his character; and ignorance is generally admitted to be a great cause of vice. If a man really understands what a bad action is, clearly perceives its *badness* and its harmful effects both upon others and upon himself, he will abstain from it, so long as that realization is vividly present to his mind. The trouble is that he does not realize what he is actually doing in committing a bad action; he does not *know* that he is sullying his own splendour and making himself a worse man. If he did, he wouldn't do it, for οὐδεὶς ἑκὼν κακός.[1] Man is so fine

[1] There can be no doubt that this is the true explanation of the Socratic doctrine that virtue is knowledge. It does not, however, take any account of the weakness of the will. I may know what is right and wish to do it, but be so dazzled, as it were, by the allurements of vice that my will refuses to obey the dictates of my intellect. Compare Ovid's famous
"Video meliora proboque;
Deteriora sequor."
Aristotle criticized the doctrine on these lines, objecting that it is disproved by the existence of incontinence or want of self-control (ἀκρασία). "But perhaps some one will raise the difficulty as to how a man who rightly comprehends can be incontinent. For some deny that the man

that—if he only realized it—no ideal is too high as a standard for his conduct; and certainly no ethical teacher has propounded a more ideal standard of morality than that to which Socrates devoted himself. His *mens conscia recti* enabled him to face death itself without a qualm; for what terrors has death for a good man? Plato, in his "Apology,"[1] represents him as concluding his defence with the following words:—

"But it is already the hour for departure, for me to go to death, for you to life. Which of the two of us goes to the better thing is unknown to all save God"—ἀλλὰ γὰρ ἤδη ὥρα ἀπιέναι, ἐμοὶ μὲν ἀποθανουμένῳ, ὑμῖν δὲ βιωσομένοις. ὁπότεροι δὲ ἡμῶν ἔρχονται ἐπὶ ἄμεινον πρᾶγμα ἄδηλον παντὶ πλὴν εἰ τῷ θεῷ. He is convinced that no calamity can befall the good man: οὐκ ἔστιν ἀνδρὶ ἀγαθῷ κακὸν οὐδὲν οὔτε ζῶντι οὔτε τελευτήσαντι" ("Apology," 41d); and so he cares for nothing in comparison with remaining ἀγαθός. To attain to such a pinnacle of independence needs a clear realization of things, long meditation in the effort to obey the old precept of γνῶθι σεαυτόν, and a right comprehension of the meaning and possibilities of

who has knowledge can be so. For it seems a monstrous thing, as Socrates held, when knowledge is in a man, for some other power to master it and drag it round like a slave. Socrates indeed was absolutely opposed to the doctrine, as though no such thing as incontinence existed; for no man with understanding acts contrary to what is best in him, but through ignorance. Now this argument is obviously at variance with the facts" (Ethics, 1145b, 21). Perhaps Socrates would have replied that in the case of the ἀκρατής the "allurements" of vice are so blinding that it is impossible to admit that ἐπιστήμη ἔνεστι, at any rate not consciously as such (ἐνεργείᾳ as Aristotle would himself say). So the Socratic doctrine may be maintained after all.

[1] The student is strongly recommended to read this dialogue in full, for no better idea of the teaching of Socrates could be derived, in any way, than what will be obtained by reading this vindication of the great master from the hand of his greatest pupil.

human life. But no man worthy of the name of man will shirk the responsibility of this investigation, for mere existence—life without reflection and examination into its meaning and possibilities—is no life for a man—ὁ γὰρ ἀνεξέταστος βίος οὐ βιωτὸς ἀνθρώπῳ (*ib.*, 38a). At such a height of moral grandeur we have no difficulty in understanding things such as the contention in the "Gorgias" that it is preferable to be the victim of injustice rather than to commit injustice (ἀδικεῖσθαι μᾶλλον ἢ ἀδικεῖν), for to suffer injustice does our own moral nature no harm, but to commit injustice is to sully our own spiritual splendour, to fall from our ideal state, to forget who we are. All this is contained in the Socratic equation of knowledge with virtue, of ἐπιστήμη with ἀρετή.

CHAPTER V

PLATO AND THE IDEALISTIC INTERPRETATION OF THE UNIVERSE

PLATO (427-347 B.C.) is the world's greatest philosopher. He was born in Athens of a noble line of ancestors, of whom he seems to have been justly proud. Upon the death of Socrates (399 B.C.) he left Athens, possibly because he could not bear to live among those who had put his master to death, and spent several years in travelling about and studying under the various men of learning in different parts of the world. Thus he is said to have lived for some years in Egypt under the instruction of the native priests; probably he also went to Italy and studied under the Pythagoreans there. After his return from his travels, he founded the famous academy at Athens, where he began to lecture. Subsequently he made two visits to Sicily, upon the invitation of Dio, who was anxious to train his nephew, Dionysius the younger, as a "philosopher-King." With this object in view he taught at Syracuse for several years, under the patronage of Dio; but the project ended in a fiasco and Plato barely escaped with his life.

His Life.

In discussing Socrates we commented upon the paramount importance of his personality. No distinction can be drawn between the personality and the doctrine of Plato; they are inextricable elements, warp and woof of the same texture.

His Personality.

When we pass to him from the pre-Socratics we feel at once the remarkable richness of his mind. "Of Plato it may justly be said that he reduced into a beautiful whole the scattered results of the earlier Greek philosophy, reconciling their seeming differences and conflicting tendencies. From this fountain, as well as from the abundant sources of his own good powers, flowed the rich elements of his philosophy. In fact, when we compare the barrenness of the earlier philosophers with the fertility of Plato, that love, which Plato knows so well how to inspire in us, warms almost to veneration; so rich, so varied, and so abundant are his observations, and so profound his knowledge of man and the world! His acquisition of these intellectual stores, however, becomes at once conceivable, if we call to mind that he had the good fortune, in the freshness and energy of youth, to fall in with a Socrates, the success of whose excellent and happy method for the improvement of man is singularly attested by the wonderful success with which he trained this his worthiest disciple to sound the innermost depth of the heart and mind, and the hidden principles of man's nature."[1] He was by no means a pure intellectualist, and contrasts, in this respect, with the much "harder" type of mind possessed by his successor Aristotle. But it is not only that, in Plato, the pure intellect was not the whole of the man; as much might be said of Epictetus; but there could be no greater contrast than exists between the somewhat unreal virtue of Epictetus, on the one hand, aloof from the world, as it were, and despising all the ills that flesh is heir to, because seclusion has made it rather etiolated, and the rich learning of Plato, on the other, throbbing with life, and full of sympathy for,

[1] Ritter's "History of Ancient Philosophy," Vol. II. p. 155 (in Morrison's translation, 1838).

and admiration of, the humanity of man. His philosophical dialogues are full of human interest. "To this Plato was led by the very form of dialogue, for, while he introduces Socrates and his contemporaries disputing and conversing, we have represented before us a progressive action of living characters; a truly dramatic group is raised before the imagination, and awakens intense and deep interest. It is to this charm of composition, no doubt, that he is indebted for many of his admirers. He is a consummate master in painting those minute traits which constantly attract and detain the reader's attention, by bringing visibly before him the peculiarities of the speakers, and by the charm of trifling incidents in advancing the progress of the dialogue; and thus does he acquire the opportunity of displaying the splendour of his eloquence, and his skill to touch the heart as well as to inform the understanding." [1]

To Plato philosophy was no narrow, departmental interest, but a speculation, as he himself describes it, upon all time and all existence—θεωρία παντὸς μὲν χρόνου, πάσης δὲ οὐσίας. And, more than this, it was not only something to be *thought*, but something to be *lived*, a way of life which gave to man, *qua* man, guidance and ideals in the direction of his intercourse with his fellows. Consequently the first step towards understanding Plato's greatness as a philosopher is to appreciate his greatness as a man.

There breathes through his dialogues a very humane spirit, a very intimate sympathy for humanity as such. When we think of him in comparison with the figures of his predecessors, we are reminded of a parallel which may be taken from the history of Greek sculpture. For, just as the representations of the gods by the great fifth-century artists seem

[1] Ritter's "History of Ancient Philosophy," Vol. II. p. 158.

somewhat cold and aloof in all the dignity and majesty of their Olympian greatness, when compared with the more kindly, almost human, benignity of, say, the Hermes of Praxiteles, or the Asclepius from Melos, so does Plato seem a warm and kindly human figure when contrasted with the rather forbidding, almost Hebrew-prophet-like, sternness of a predecessor such as Empedocles.

<small>The Introductions to the Dialogues.</small>

Homo sum, nihil humani alienum a me puto is as applicable to Plato as to anyone. Hence the delightful introductions to his dialogues, in which, before the philosophical argument is begun, we are given a very real and very human setting to the conversation which is to follow. And with a few masterful strokes—for Plato is a great artist—he will give us the character and tone, as it were, of the *dramatis personæ*, so that we are enabled to give the more significance to the respective doctrines soon to be maintained—much in the same way as Thomas Hardy brings us straight into the atmosphere of his novels by introducing a character walking along a lonely country road, generally in the evening, passing, or being overtaken by, one of those familiar carrier's carts, so that we are in the mood to *feel* the character before a single word has been spoken. Similarly the little introductions in Plato are not irrelevant to the philosophical argument which is to follow; they are as essential for the right attuning of our minds to Plato's conception of what philosophy is, as is the literal tuning of his instrument in the musician's hands before he begins his piece. This will be obvious from a consideration of the "setting of the stage" preparatory to the long dialogue of the "Republic."

Yesterday I went down to the Piræus with Glaucon, son of Ariston, to pray to the goddess, and also because I wished to view the festival, and to see how it was celebrated, as it was to be held for the first time.

I thought the procession of the natives of Athens was pretty, but that of the Thracians pleased me no less. When we had prayed and looked on, we left to go back to the city, but Polemarchus, the son of Cephalus, noticed us from a distance, wending our way homeward, and told his slave to run and to ask us to wait for him. So the servant, coming up behind me, took hold of my cloak and said, "Polemarchus asks you to wait for him." Then I turned round and asked where his master was. "That is he," he replied, "coming along behind. Will you wait for him?"—"We will wait for him," Glaucon answered. Soon after Polemarchus came up, and with him Adeimantus, the brother of Glaucon, and Niceratus the son of Nicias, and several other men, apparently coming from the procession. Polemarchus said, "Well, Socrates, you two seem to me to be leaving and making for the city."— "You are quite right," I answered. "Now you see how many of us there are?" said he.—"I do." "Well," he said, "either prove yourselves our masters, or stay here."—"But there is still an alternative left," I replied. "What if we persuade you that you ought to let us go?" "But could you persuade us when we will not listen?"—"Certainly not!" answered Glaucon. "Well, we are not going to listen; you may as well understand that." Then Adeimantus said, "Do you not know that there will be a torch-race on horseback in the evening, in the celebration of the goddess?"—"On horseback?" I cried. "That is something new. Will they have torches in their hands, and pass them on one to the other, while the horses are galloping?" I asked.— "Yes," answered Polemarchus, "and besides this there will be a night festival worth seeing. We will rise after dinner and go to see the night festival; there we will meet many of our young friends, with whom we will converse. So please stay, and do as we ask." Then Glaucon said, "It seems as if we will have to stay."—"Well," I answered, "if you wish we will do so." We went home therefore with Polemarchus, and there we found Lysias and Euthydemus, the brothers of Polemarchus, and also Thrasymachus of Chalcedon and Charmantides of Pæania and Cleitophon, son of Aristonymus. Cephalus, the father of Polemarchus, was also at home; and he seemed quite aged to me, for it was a long time since I had seen him. He was sitting on a chair with a cushion, and on his head he had a chaplet, for he had just been sacrificing in the courtyard. We seated ourselves by him, as there were chairs ranged round him in a circle. The moment Cephalus saw me, he greeted me and said, "You do not often visit us at the Piræus, Socrates. You have no excuse. If my strength would allow me to walk to the city with ease, you would not need to come here, but we would visit you. As it is, however, you ought to come here more often. For I tell you, the more all the pleasures of the body waste away, the more my desire for intellectual discussion and my delight in it increases. So do as I ask you, and spend your time with these young men, and come to visit us here as we are most intimate friends."—"Indeed, Cephalus," I replied, "I find great pleasure in conversing with old people. Since they have passed along a road which we too perhaps will have to follow, I think we ought to discover what it is like, whether it is rough and hard, or easy and smooth of passage. Now I, for my part, would be glad to learn from you what your opinion is, now that you are, as the poets say, on the threshold of old age, whether this period of life is hard, or what your report of it is."—"Yes, indeed, Socrates, I will tell you what it seems like to me. Often several of us who are nearly of the same age, bearing out the old proverb, gather together. And when we are met, most of them lament because they miss the pleasures of youth, and call to mind their love affairs, their drinking parties, their feastings, and suchlike, and they are vexed because they imagine they have lost great advantages, saying that then they lived well, but now they do not even live at all. Some of them bewail the insults of their relatives cast at their old age, and on this score they reproach old age as the cause of so many ills. But I think, Socrates, that these men do not blame the right thing. For if old age were to blame, then I too would have suffered these very things, and so would all men who have reached this stage of life. As it is, however, I have met others who did not hold this view, and in particular the poet Sophocles, who, while I was present, was asked by somebody, 'What do you think about love now, Sophocles? Are you still able to love a woman?'—He answered, 'Hush! my friend. I am most glad to say I have escaped from it, as I would from a raving, savage master.' I thought then, and none the less now, that he spoke wisely. For in old age comes complete peace and deliverance from such things. For when lust strains no longer and looses its grip, then the saying of Sophocles comes true. It is indeed like deliverance from a great number of raving masters. Of such things, and of the suffering caused by their relatives, there is but one cause, not old age, Socrates, but the men's disposition. For if they are orderly and easy-tempered, old age is no excessive trouble. But if not, such men find both old age and youth painful."

I admired what he had said, and as I wished him to continue, I tried to move him by saying, "O Cephalus, I think that when you say such things, the majority of men do not agree with you, but believe that you

IDEALISTIC INTERPRETATION OF UNIVERSE

bear old age easily, not through your disposition, but because you possess great wealth. For the rich, they say, have many comforts."—"What you say is true," he answered, "they do not agree with me; and there is something in what they say, but not all they imagine. There was wisdom in the reply of Themistocles who in answer to a man of Seriphus who was railing at him, saying that he owed his fame to his country and not to himself, said that if he himself were a native of Seriphus, he would not have become famous, nor would the other had he been an Athenian. This saying applies equally to those who are not rich, and do not bear old age easily, for a good man could not bear old age with much ease under stress of poverty, nor could a bad man, though rich, be at ease with himself." "Did you inherit the greater part of your wealth, or gain it, Cephalus?" I asked.—"Did I gain it, Socrates? As far as money-making goes, I come in between my grandfather and my father. For my grandfather, whose name is the same as mine, inherited almost the same amount of wealth as I now possess, and made it many times as great; but my father, Lysanias, made it even smaller than it is now. I am content if I leave it to these sons of mine not smaller, but, if possible, a little larger than when I inherited it." "The reason I asked you," I said, "was that you did not seem to me to think highly of wealth. This is usually done by those who have not acquired it themselves; those on the other hand who have acquired it are twice as fond of it again as anybody else. For just as poets love their own poems, and fathers their own children, in the same way those who have made money care for their wealth, not only as others do because of its use, but also because it is a work of their own. On this account it is unpleasant to associate with them, since they praise nothing else but money."—"Quite true," said he. "It certainly is," I answered, "but answer me this too. What do you consider the greatest advantage you have enjoyed through your wealth?"—"If I told that, probably few would believe me. Let me inform you, Socrates, that when a man almost imagines that his end is at hand, fear comes upon him and concern about things which before affected him not. For those well-known stories about Hades, how he who in this life commits injustice must there be punished, which before he mocked at, now trouble his soul for fear they be true. And now whether through the weakness of old age, or because he is very near the things that are to be, he perceives them more clearly. Thus he becomes full of apprehension and fear, and reckons up and considers whether in some way he has wronged somebody. Then he who discovers in his life a multitude of unjust acts wakes suddenly out of his sleep, as children do, and is terrified and lives with the expectation of evil. But he who is conscious that there is no injustice in him is accompanied ever by sweet hope, 'the kindly nourisher of old age,' as Pindar says. Yes, it was charmingly said by him of the man who passes his life in justness and holiness, that 'sweet hope is ever with him fostering his heart, the nourisher of old age, hope which above all governs the changeful mind of mortal man.' It is true, wonderfully true. And it is with reference to this that I state that wealth is most valuable, I do not say to everybody, but to the good. For it plays a great part in saving us from unwilling trickery and deceit, from owing sacrifices to the gods or money to men and from going to the next world in fear. It has many other uses too. But when I weigh one thing against another, I would hold that it is with reference to this that wealth is most useful to a sensible man." "You have spoken wonderfully well, Cephalus," I said. "But this justice that you mention are we to call it simply truth, and the paying back of what one receives, or is it possible for the very same acts to be sometimes just, sometimes unjust? This is what I mean. Everybody would agree that if a man receives weapons from a friend in his senses, when the same friend is mad and asks them back, he ought not to return such things, nor would he be acting justly if he did, or told the whole truth to a man in such a state."—"What you say is true," he answered. "Then truth and the paying back of what one receives is not the definition of justice."—"But it is indeed," interrupted Polemarchus, "if we are to believe Simonides." "Well," said Cephalus, "I will pass the discussion on to you. It is time for me to look after the sacrifices." "Then," said I, "is Polemarchus the heir to your part in it?"—"Yes," he answered, with a smile, and went away to the sacrifices (327a-331d9).

Visualization of the dialogi personæ.

Sometimes at a lull in the argument, or when one aspect of the case has been finished with—when one or other of the interlocutors has been hopelessly defeated by Socrates in his untiring play of question and answer—we are once more brought back, for a moment, to a visualization of the characters as living human beings. This serves partly as a relief to the strenuous intellectual effort of following the argument—a relief which we may compare with that which Shakespeare gives us by interposing a comic episode (e.g. the porter scene in "Macbeth") at one of the most intense points in his tragedies,

—but it is much more part and parcel of Plato's whole conception of philosophy as a living matter. The introductions first bring the characters before us, and although, of course, they live and unfold themselves, as it were, in the disquisitions which follow, these little interludes, in which we see the participants shifting their positions and re-settling themselves in the circle of disputants before the next round of argument begins, do serve largely to keep up our realization of them as men, to keep them before us as living beings. Thus in the first book of the "Republic," upon the conclusion of the first round between Socrates and Polemarchus on the Simonidean definition of justice as the rendering of what is due—τὸ τὰ ὀφειλόμενα ἑκάστῳ ἀποδιδόναι—the interruption of Thrasymachus provides an occasion upon which we can see all the disputants sitting round spell-bound and not a little disconcerted at the brusqueness of Thrasymachus' manner :—

> Very often while we were conversing, Thrasymachus attempted to interrupt us in the middle of our discussion in order to make an objection, but he was restrained by those who were sitting around, because they were eager to hear the discussion right to the end. But when we paused and I had finished saying these things, he could keep quiet no longer, but gathering himself together like a wild beast he hurled himself upon us, as if with the intent of tearing us to pieces. I and Polemarchus were startled and panic-stricken; then Thrasymachus bawling out in the middle of us all said, "What nonsense has taken hold of you two all this time, Socrates? Why do you play the fool together, and give way thus one to the other? If as you say you do indeed wish to know what justice is, do not only ask questions and pride yourself thus upon your refutations, when anybody gives an answer, because you know well that it is easier to ask questions than to answer them; but answer yourself too and tell us what you think justice is; and be careful not to define it as what is binding, or advantageous, or profitable, or gainful, or expedient, but tell me clearly and exactly whatever you have to say; and be sure I will not accept what you say if you talk such rubbish." When I heard this I was amazed, and looked on him with fear, and had I not set eyes on him before he

looked at me I believe I should have been dumb. As it was, however, when he first began to be exasperated by the discussion, I had glanced at him the first so that I was able to answer him, and said not without trembling, "Oh, Thrasymachus, do not be hard on us. If I and my friend here have made mistakes in our consideration of the question; be assured that they were quite unintended. You do not imagine if we were looking for a gold coin that we would voluntarily give way one to the other in our search and destroy our chances of discovering it; and now that we are searching after justice, a thing more precious than many coins of gold, do not imagine that we would thus foolishly give way to each other, instead of taking great pains to discover it, do not imagine that, my friend. But my opinion is that it is beyond us. Therefore it is more meet that we should be pitied, rather than sternly treated, by such wonderful men as you." On hearing this he burst out laughing very mockingly and said, "Oh, Hercules! here you see that affected ignorance of Socrates. I knew it, and warned those present that you would not wish to answer, but would affect ignorance and do anything but reply when asked a question."—"You are wise, Thrasymachus," I answered : " thus you knew well that if you asked a man what makes twelve, and at the same time warned him, 'Now, my friend, take care not to say that twice six is twelve, or three times four, or six times two, or four times three; because be sure I shall not accept what you say if you talk any such nonsense.' It was clear to you, I suppose, that nobody would answer such a question. But if he answered you thus, 'Oh! Thrasymachus, what do you mean? Even if one of these is the answer, am I, my dear sir, to say something else which is not in accordance with the truth? Is this what you mean?' What would you say to him then?"—"Very good," said he; "as if there is any similarity between this case and that."—"There is nothing to prevent it," I answered. "But even if there is no similarity, if it appears some such thing to the man questioned, do you think he is any the less likely to answer what appears right to him, whether we forbid it or not?"— "Do you mean that this is what you will do? Will you give as an answer one of the things which I have banned?"—"I should not wonder," I replied, "if it seemed right to me after consideration."— "What then, said he, "if I show you another answer about justice different from all these and better than them? What do you deserve to suffer?" —"What else," I answered, "if not that which it befits the ignorant to suffer? That is to learn from the man who does know. This, therefore, is what I too deserve to suffer."—"You are an engaging person," he said. "But, besides learning, you must pay some money as well,"

IDEALISTIC INTERPRETATION OF UNIVERSE

—" Yes, when I have some," I replied.—" But you have," cried Glaucon. " Now speak for money, Thrasymachus, for we will all contribute to Socrates."—" Of course," he answered, " so that Socrates, I suppose, in his usual manner may not answer himself, but may catch up and refute the answers of somebody else."—" My worthy friend," I answered, " how can a man answer who in the first place does not know and confesses that he does not, and if he has any ideas on the subject is forbidden by one not to be despised, to say what he thinks? It is your place rather to speak. For you say that you know, and have something to say. So do not refuse, but please me by answering, and do not grudge to teach Glaucon here and these others." When I had spoken thus, Glaucon and the others begged him not to decline. Thrasymachus obviously longed to speak so as to gain glory, for he thought he had a beautiful answer, but he pretended to contend to make me the one to answer. Finally he yielded and said, " This, then, is the wisdom of Socrates, to refuse to teach himself, and to go about learning from others, and then not even to return thanks for what he learns."— " When you say I learn from others, Thrasymachus, you speak the truth; but when you say I do not return thanks, you speak falsely. For I pay requital in so far as I can. I can give praise alone, for I have no money. But with what readiness I do this, if I think a person has spoken wisely, you will soon know for yourself, when you have spoken. For I feel sure that you will speak wisely."—" Then listen," he answered. " My opinion is that justice is nothing else than the interest of the stronger. Why do you not praise me? But you will refuse " (" Republic," 336b1-338c3).

It is this human element in Plato that particularly distinguishes him from his great successor Aristotle. It has been said that every man is either a Platonist or an Aristotelian, and although it will be pointed out in this survey that there is more of what we may provisionally call idealism in Aristotle than is often imagined, it yet remains true that with him the "thought" element predominates over "feeling;" the intellectual side of man's nature tends to confine, if it does not entirely eliminate, the emotional. Whereas with Plato this is by no means the case; with him the "feeling" element is as great as is the "thought" element, *Thought and Feeling.*

and he produces in us the conviction that with him "feeling" comes in as a sort of guarantee, as it were, of the rightness of "thought," not an alien feeling of satisfaction superinduced ὥσπερ περίαπτόν τι, as Aristotle would say, upon the intellectual conviction, but a feeling of moral enthusiasm suffusing the whole discussion. This is why, in discussing such abstract moral qualities as justice and injustice, for example, he will often throw abstractions overboard, as though it were that he feared otherwise to lose something of the real significance of such qualities in their human values.[1] To bring out the real significance of these qualities, he brings the just and the unjust *man* vividly before our eyes. In the "Gorgias," for example, Polus gives a very lurid description of the excesses of Archelaus, tyrant of Macedonia, as though unlimited power meant unlimited happiness; but the picture is so drawn that Socrates finds it an easy task to convince Polus that no man, who is such as Archelaus has been described to be, can for a moment be thought happy. He simply asks Polus whether he considers the Archelaus, whom he has described, to be a just or an unjust man. Polus admits that he is ἄδικος,[2] and then Socrates proves, in accordance with his own moral teaching (see above, p. 68), that no ἄδικος can possibly be εὐδαίμων, and that it is better ἀδικεῖσθαι ἢ ἀδικεῖν.

Concrete Instances to "clinch" Abstract Principles.

Vivid descriptions. Another outstanding element in the style of Plato is his love of vivid descriptions. We think of his description of

---

[1] Compare the remark about justice in "Republic," 432d: "My good sir, it seems to have been rolling before our feet right from the beginning, and we did not see it, but were in a most ridiculous plight. Just as men sometimes search for what they hold in their hands, so we did not cast our eyes upon it, but kept our gaze upon some distant object, in doing which it has perhaps escaped our notice."

[2] The English word *unrighteous* corresponds rather better than *unjust* to the connotation of the Greek word.

IDEALISTIC INTERPRETATION OF UNIVERSE

the "business man" (ὁ χρηματιστής) stooping in his walk and pretending not even to see the man whom he has swindled, and of all those many concrete instances of cobblers, potters, bridle-makers, and what not. But two short quotations must suffice. In the "Republic" (361e) Glaucon has been maintaining that it pays to be unjust—it is the old complaint that the wicked prosper and the good suffer in this world—and in order to "draw" Socrates he tells him of the many occasions upon which he has heard injustice, in effect, belauded, inasmuch as it is appearances that count; it matters not to *be* just, but only to *appear* so, and these are the vivid words which he puts into the mouths of the eulogists of appearances :—

> They will tell you this, that the just man who is so conditioned (i.e. thought unjust) will be scourged, crucified, cast into chains, will have his eyes burnt out, and finally, after undergoing all kinds of suffering, will be impaled and so brought to understand that his desire should be to seem just, and not to be so. In fact the words of Æschylus were far more applicable to the unjust, than to the just, man. For they will say that the unjust man, in so far as he is pursuing something real and not living with a view to appearances, really wants to be unjust and not merely to seem so;
>
>> "And from the culture of his modest worth
>> Bears the rich fruit of great and glorious deeds."[1]
>
> For, firstly, he is thought just and so rules in the city, then he can marry from whatsoever family he chooses; he can give in marriage to whomsoever he likes, can enter into contracts and partnerships at will, and always to his own profit, taking advantage of the fact that his conscience is not worried about injustice. When he enters into any competition either public or private he always gets the better of his rival and proves the superior, and as a result he becomes wealthy and can serve his friends and injure his enemies; he can give adequate and magnificent sacrifices and offerings to the gods, and so curry favour much better than the just man with whomsoever he wishes either of

---

[1] Æschylus, "Seven against Thebes," 593.

gods or of men, so it is only reasonable to suppose that he, rather than the just man, is the more beloved of heaven."[1]

In a later passage of the "Republic"[2] Socrates replies to all this in no less vivid language :—

You must let me now say of them (i.e. the just) all that you yourself were saying about the unjust. For I shall say that the just, when they grow up, hold office in their own cities, if so they choose, marry from whatsoever family they desire, and give in marriage wherever they like. And all that you said about the others, I now say about these. And, on the other hand, I say of the unjust that the majority of them, even if they escape in youth, are caught at the end of their course and look foolish, and when they become old are subjected to wretched insults at the hands of strangers and citizens alike, being scourged and subjected to all those things which you rightly declared were unfit for polite ears to listen to—they will be crucified and burnt—but imagine that you have heard the full description of their sufferings from me.

The Philosopher. But, fond as he is of such concrete instances, of thus bringing vividly before our eyes the particular manifestations of some general principle, Plato never "fails to see the wood for the trees." He takes the particular instance partly, no doubt, because it is a check upon those airy nothings to which abstract philosophical speculation is only too prone, but it is with him always not merely *particular;* it is an *instance*, symbolical, as it were, of something beyond itself. As Aristotle would say, Plato sees the universal in the particular;[3] with something of the poet's vision he passes beyond the mere phenomena and sees in them the embodiment of eternal principles. Lovers of Wordsworth are well acquainted with this power of quiet contemplation, when things are seen for what they really are by the "inward eye" of the soul so that

---

[1] "Republic," 361e.   [2] 613d.
[3] In fact, none of his "particular instances" is a mere τόδε τι, it is always a τοιόνδε τι.

the meanest thing (or flower) can bring "thoughts that do often lie too deep for tears." And the case is the same with Plato; for, just as Wordsworth has been criticized for dealing so much with common things—and often, it must be confessed, he fails to make us see all that he, no doubt, saw himself in those "common things,"—so we can well believe that Plato's preoccupation with common things—the young Socrates in the "Parmenides"[1] speaks of mud, hair, and dirt—was a thing which many of his disciples could not understand: the reason being that, as Parmenides says to the youthful Socrates, they were young and had not yet got that grasp of philosophy which later life brings, when a man despises nothing, whereas in youth a man judges of things according to the prevalent opinions of those around him. The philosopher despises nothing, simply because he sees in it more than others, for whom it has "faded into the light of common day," can possibly see. And Plato *always* sees things thus, it is inevitable in him, for it is part of his mental vision. It is at the bottom of his "Doctrine of Ideas," the *fons et origo* of what we shall come to understand as his μίμησις theory.[2] But we are concerned with it here generally, and not merely as the explanation of some particular Platonic doctrine. It is what, with Plato, makes philosophy no abstract speculation, but a living thing—something that touches the very heart of life. In this connexion we may quote what R. L. Nettleship[3] has said: "Philosophy to most of us is too much wrapt up in the associations of books and systems, of technicalities and jargon, to let us feel the living spirit which it still is when it is anything more than a set of phrases. And the love of truth, in spite of the boasts of modern

[1] 130c.   [2] See below, p. 108.
[3] Essay on "The Republic of Plato," in "Hellenica," p. 77.

science, is still but rarely found to dominate the character and mould the life, as Plato conceived that it might do. . . . When he spoke of 'the truth,' or of 'what is,' we see that there entered into his feeling not only the enthusiasm of the scientific discoverer, but also the passion of the poet for beauty and the devotion of the saint to the object of his worship." Plato himself describes the philosopher as one who has no concern with earthly matters as such; is never filled with malice or envy in strife against men. His eye is always looking to fixed, immutable principles which he sees neither suffering nor causing injury to one another, but always regulated in order according to reason. So he tries to adapt himself to these principles, and mould his character in accordance with them; for he cannot help wanting to make himself like what he admires so much—ἢ οἴει τινὰ μηχανὴν εἶναι, ὅτῳ τις ὁμιλεῖ ἀγάμενος, μὴ μιμεῖσθαι ἐκεῖνο;[1] with us the "love of truth" is a phrase; with Plato it was, as love should be, a passion; his philosophic impulse is an ideal enthusiasm for the things of the mind and of the soul; it makes him one of those "lords of philosophy" who, as he says in the "Theætetus,"

have never from their youth upward known the way to the marketplace, nor where the law courts are, or the council chamber, or where any other municipal assembly is held. They neither see nor hear the laws or decrees of the State recited or written; the seeking of office by political organizations, meetings and dinners and revels with singing maidens are things which never come into their minds even in dreams. Whether any city affair has turned out well or ill, what scandal has befallen a man from his ancestry, either male or female, are things of which he knows no more than he knows—as the saying goes—how many pints the sea contains. Nor is he aware of his ignorance. For he does not neglect these things for the sake of being thought a fine man, but because, as a matter of fact, it is only his outward form that is

---

[1] "Republic," 500c.

dwelling in the city. His mind, thinking all these things of small or of no account, and consequently despising them, is " flying all around," as Pindar says, " above the world " measuring all things on earth and " in the heavens above," examining the whole nature of each and all, but not lending itself to anything lowly at hand.[1]

It is this impassioned contemplation—when only the " outward form " of the philosopher is " in the city "—that constitutes the real philosophic impulse, which, beginning with our natural love of beauty, of fair forms, leads us on to see the beauty of the mind, until we finally attain satisfaction in the contemplation of Truth ; for, as Keats tells us,

Ἔρως as Philosophic Impulse.

> Beauty is truth, truth beauty ; that is all
> Ye know on earth, and all ye need to know.—

the best commentary upon which is to be found in the " Symposium."

Now he who would pursue this matter aright ought from his earliest youth to begin to visit beautiful forms, and at first, if his instructor guides him aright, he should love one form only and there generate beauteous thoughts ; then he should realize that the beauty which appears in one form is brother to the beauty in another form ; then if it is beauty in general that he must seek, it would be the height of folly not to realize that the beauty of all forms is one and the same thing. When he has perceived this he will make himself a lover of all beautiful forms, and slackening his love for the one form, he will contemn it and think it a small thing. After this he should consider the beauty of the soul a more precious thing than the beauty of the form, so that him who has a sweet soul but little bloom of form he will be content to love and cherish, and to create and search for those thoughts by which the young are improved ; and thence he will be compelled to perceive the beauty of laws and pursuits, and to realize the fact that all this beauty is akin, and accordingly to think but little of the beauty of the form. After pursuits he should be introduced to the sciences, so that he may see the beauty of knowledge too ; and, looking on a wide beauty, no longer will he, like a slave, be held in love by the beauty of one thing, of one boy, or man, or pursuit, and in his enslavement become paltry and mean of mind, but turning to the wide sea of beauty and contemplating it he

---

[1] "Theætetus, 173d.

will give birth to many lovely and ennobling thoughts and notions, in bounteous love of wisdom; until thus strengthened and increased he will survey one science, which is the science of universal beauty. Now, he said, try to attend to me as keenly as you can. He who has received guidance thus far towards the things of love, and has contemplated beautiful things aright and in due order, as he arrives at the end of these things on a sudden he beholds a beauty of wondrous nature, the very thing, Socrates, which was the end of all his former labours, a beauty which in the first place is eternal, which is not produced nor destroyed, which waxes not and wanes not, which is not beautiful in one way and deformed in another, nor sometimes beautiful and at other times not, nor beautiful in one respect and deformed in another, nor beautiful in one place and in another deformed, beautiful in the opinion of some and deformed in the opinion of others; nor can it be accorded beauty in the likeness of a face or of hands, or of any other portion of the body, nor of speech, nor of a science, nor does it exist in any other thing, as in an animal, or in the earth or sky or any other thing, but it is very beauty by itself and of itself, it is of one form and endures for ever, of such a nature that, as all the other things of beauty which participate in it are created or destroyed, it does not itself become either greater or less, but suffers in no way. Now when a man through being taught to love aright, starting from these things of beauty and ascending, begins to gaze upon this beauty, he has almost reached the goal. For this is the true way to approach the things of love, or to be guided there by another, beginning from these things of beauty to ascend for the sake of that one beauty, ascending, as on steps, from one thing of beauty to two, and from two to all beautiful forms, and from beautiful forms to beautiful pursuits, and from beautiful pursuits to beautiful sciences, until from these sciences he comes finally to that science which is nothing else than the science of beauty itself, and comprehends the essence of beauty. This life, my dear Socrates, said the stranger of Mantineia, above all others should be lived by man, a life spent in the contemplation of beauty itself. And this beauty, if ever you see it, will not appear to you as gold and raiment, and lovely boys and youths on whom you now gaze with admiration, and are prepared, both you and others, to look on and be with, and, if it were possible, neither to eat nor drink if only you could gaze on them and be their companions. What if man perchance could see absolute beauty, clear, pure, and uncontaminated, not filled out with fleshly and mortal things, and colours, and all the inanities of mortality, but to gaze on the divine beauty itself in its one form? Is that man's life unworthy, think you, who gazes thus, and contemplates and dwells with that which is befitting? Do you not think that there alone he will be able to see beauty as it may be seen, to create not shadows of virtue, but realities, since he holds reality and not a shadow, and by producing and nourishing true virtue to become a friend of the gods and, if any human man gains such a gift, immortal. These are the things, Phædrus and all you others, which Diotima told, and which I believe to be true (210a-212a).

This high ideal of the life of the φιλόσοφος implies an ἐπιστήμη equally high ideal of ἐπιστήμη or scientific knowledge. This is opposed to mere opinion (δόξα); and, even if that opinion happens to be correct (ὀρθὴ δόξα), it is still inferior to ἐπιστήμη, in that it is, as it were, a mere isolated fragment of knowledge, not realized in its context, and discerned by the clear light of reason as an eternal truth, bound αἰτίας λογισμῷ with the whole system of our human knowledge, grasped as an immutable principle, and viewed, as Spinoza would say, *sub specie æternitatis*. Such knowledge as this is no mere "instruction" or "learning"; just as we make a distinction to-day between the man who "knows a lot" and the man who is really educated, between the acquisition of information and the enriching of the spirit, so in Platonic language ἐπιστήμη has nothing to do with πολυμαθία; it is something which when attained affects and deepens a man's whole nature; it may not extend over a wide field but it goes deep; the line upon which it moves is vertical and not horizontal.

It has its counterpart in the practical sphere; for what Σωφρο-
ἐπιστήμη is in intellectual speculation σωφροσύνη is in the σύνη.
sphere of conduct; the one is clear understanding of an abstract principle as an eternal and immutable law of the universe, the other is clear understanding of a concrete action as an unfailing index of what we are ourselves.

"I should certainly maintain," says Charmides, in the dialogue that bears his name, "that temperance is just this—knowledge of oneself—

and I agree with him who dedicated this remark at Delphi. For I think that the dedication of the remark is meant as a salutation from the god to those who enter the temple—instead of the usual 'Hail'— since the salutation of 'Hail' is not a right one, and we should not greet one another thus, but bid each other to 'be temperate.' And so it is that the god addresses those who enter his temple with a greeting different from that of men—such was the idea, I think, in the mind of the dedicator. And he accosts each worshipper as he enters the temple with no other greeting than this of 'Be temperate!' But he expresses himself in riddles like a seer; for 'Know thyself' and 'Be temperate' are one and the same thing, as the inscription indicates and I maintain, but others may think them different, as I think is the case with those who dedicated the later inscriptions of 'Nothing in excess,' and 'Evil follows on a pledge,' for they took 'Know thyself' as a piece of advice and not the salutation of the god to those who entered his temple" (164d).

From such quotations the reader will perceive how Plato's ethical teaching permeates the whole of his writings. We will not, therefore, give a separate section upon his ethics, his definition of δικαιοσύνη [1]—the ostensible subject of inquiry in the "Republic"—but take up one or two aspects of his teaching which more readily lend themselves to separate treatment.

I. The Psychology of Plato.

I. Psychology

It is usual to speak of the "tripartite division of the soul" in Plato ; but we must never forget that such a division does

---

[1] It is given as τὸ τὰ αὑτοῦ πράττειν καὶ μὴ πολυπραγμονεῖν (" Republic," 433a)—in vulgar parlance " Mind your own business," but in Plato denoting a realization of oneself as, on the one hand, a *man* (i.e. capable of the highest activities of mind and soul) and, on the other, as a member of a community with both rights and duties in reference to others. It is that " social conscience " without which no organized society is possible ; it is not even so definite a *thing* as are the virtues of σωφροσύνη, ἀνδρεία, and φρόνησις, but rather that which makes possible the realization of these—ὃ πᾶσιν ἐκείνοις τὴν δύναμιν παρέσχεν ὥστε ἐγγενέσθαι, καὶ ἐγγενομένοις γε σωτηρίαν παρέχειν, ἕωσπερ ἂν ἐνῇ (433c).

not imply any actual division of the soul into three separate parts or faculties; the whole soul is involved, and as it were functions, in all our acts, whether they come within the lowest or the highest category in the scale of worth. In a word, the division is purely logical, made for the sake of convenience of presentation. These three "parts" are

1. τὸ ἐπιθυμητικὸν μέρος or ἐπιθυμία (desire or appetite).
2. τὸ θυμοειδές or θυμός (spirit, or the sense of honour).
3. τὸ λογιστικὸν μέρος (the rational element).

These are often referred to by different names in different passages of Plato's writings, but the above are the most representative terms. By ἐπιθυμία he means the desire of satisfying some natural appetite—it is usually confined either to the things of the body, such as food and drink, or to the material "good things" of the world, summed up, in the case of man, under the desire for wealth—which is common to man and beast alike.[1] The second "part" is something superior to this. It is fostered and stimulated by hard athletic exercise, and corresponds, in some at least, of its aspects, to that "pluck" or "grit" which it is the claim of our modern public-school education to develop by the prominence which it gives to games. The λογιστικὸν μέρος is the highest development of the soul, that which is concerned with art, science, and literature. Plato expounds this doctrine under the figure of a tripartite monster which is thus built up : after suggesting the analogy between such an image and the human soul, Socrates, in the "Republic," replies to the question as to what kind of an image he has in mind, as follows :—

One of that kind of creatures, said I, which are fabled to have been of old, such as the Chimaira, Scylla, and Cerberus, and others where many forms grew and combined together into one.

[1] It thus corresponds to Aristotle's αἰσθητικὴ ζωή (see below, p. 118).

There are such fables, said he.

Now mould the one form of a many-headed manifold beast, which has in a circle the heads of tame animals and wild animals, and which is able to put forth from itself and vary all these at will.

It is the work of a marvellous moulder, said he, but, as a story is more easily fashioned than wax and such substances, let it be moulded.

Now mould the form of a lion, and another form of a man, but let the first form be far the largest, and the second be second.

These two are easier, said he. They are moulded. Now fix the three together into one, so that they all grow together.

I have fixed them together, said he.

Last of all mould around them on the outside the form of one of them, that of the man, so that to one who is unable to see the inside, but who can see only the outside covering, it may appear to be one animal, a man.

I have moulded it around, he answered.

And now to the one who affirms that it is profitable for man to act unjustly, but that to be just does not benefit him, let us reply that he says nothing more nor less than that it is profitable for him to feast the manifold beast and make it strong, along with the lion and all its parts, but to starve the man to death and make him weak, so that he is dragged about wherever either of the others leads him, and makes no attempt to accustom the one to the other, or to make them pleasing to each other, but allows them to bite and fight among themselves, and devour each other.

Yes, he said, the man who praises injustice will be saying that exactly.

Again, would not he who says that justice is profitable, say that everything should be done, and everything said, to the end that the inner man may have the fullest command over the whole man, and look after the many-headed beast, like a farmer, nursing and domesticating the tame parts, and preventing the wild parts from growing: and with the lion as an ally, caring for each and all in common, making them friendly to each other and to himself, is it not thus that he will rear them?

That is exactly what he who praises justice says.

So in every way he who praises justice will speak the truth, but he who praises injustice will lie. For when one considers either pleasure or fame, or advantage, he who praises justice speaks the truth, but he who blames it, knows nothing, and his blaming is in no way sound ("Republic," 588d).

In figures of this nature in Plato every detail has its significance; he never fills out the picture from the mere exuberance of imagination. The first " multitudinous beast " —which represents ἐπιθυμία—has many heads, because "desire" is itself manifold; it runs first after this and then after that, without any controlling element to bring its erratic impulses to subserve one abiding purpose, to bring them, as we say, to a head. It is always thinking—in so far as it "thinks" at all—that it is going to attain happiness by *this* indulgence; it fails, and so it tries the other; *that* too fails, and so it tries a third, and so on. Wherefore it is represented with many heads. The second, or "lion," part is smaller than the first, although larger than the third, or purely human, part. This means that τὸ θυμοειδές is an element of the soul which has, in size, no comparison with the unrestricted field over which the uncontrolled passions and appetites of man are so liable to stray; but it is larger than τὸ λογιστικόν, for many men have a "sense of honour," but comparatively few reach the heights among which Plato places the finest concerns of man. And notice what is described as the peculiar function of the third or highest part. It has to govern "the many-headed monster," for we must control our appetites and not be carried away by them; we must bring them into order and make them subserve the dominating ideal of our lives, or they will rush us hither and thither aimlessly through the world. This highest part of the soul is, roughly speaking, what we commonly mean by the word *soul* in everyday, non-philosophical language; it is that which gives man his real significance, distinguishes him from the beasts, and constitutes his kinship with the divine, for it is the part of man which is immortal. Plato generally puts his doctrine about it under the guise of myth (see below, p. 97); but it is the subject of that last discourse of Socrates in prison, which is described so vividly in the "Phædo," where we find Socrates describing the hindrance which the body is to the soul[1] in the pursuit of knowledge and the release which death will bring from all such trammels.

II. POLITICS

II. The Politics of Plato. Anyone who has studied the barest elements of philology will be acquainted with the way in which a single word often bears silent witness to the degeneration of man or of society; and the word "politics" is a notable example of this. Trench's "Study of Words" abounds with such examples (e.g. "villain," "rival," etc.), and, whatever the cause of this so-called "pejorative tendency,"[2] there can be no doubt that "politics" generally means to us to-day something very different from what ἡ πολιτική—the science of statesmanship —meant for Plato. His political ideals are set forth in the "Republic" under the form of a description of an imaginary commonwealth, such as is familiar to English readers from William Morris's "News from Nowhere," or Butler's "Erewhon," or H. G. Wells's "Modern Utopia[3]—the last

---

[1] Cf. "Gorgias," 492-3, where he quotes with approval Euripides'
τίς δ' οἶδεν εἰ τὸ ζῆν μέν ἐστι κατθανεῖν,
τὸ κατθανεῖν δὲ ζῆν ;
and says that the body is, as it were, the tomb of the soul—τὸ μὲν σῶμά ἐστιν ἡμῖν σῆμα.

[2] Perhaps it should be mentioned that more recent writers on the subject object to this tracing of "tendencies" in words themselves; the causes for the changes in the meaning of words should be found rather in the predispositions of our own human nature (e.g. the natural desire to avoid giving offence, human malice, euphemism, etc.). See Bréal's "Semantics," chapter ix. (English translation by Mrs. Henry Cust).

[3] The idea is common, and there are many earlier examples in English Literature ; cf. Bacon's " New Atlantis," Hobbes's " Leviathan," More's " Utopia."

of which indeed would seem to have borrowed a good deal from Plato.

Plato is led to describe his ideal State as a result of the desire to define δικαιοσύνη, for it is in the ideal State, if anywhere, that Justice will be found; and it is one of Plato's deepest convictions that it is a mistake to try to determine any moral quality in the abstract, apart from its context in the life of man. So we must consider the conditions, the environment, necessary to the development and fullest manifestation of τὸ λογιστικόν—the highest psychic "part" —in the individual. This ideal State—called πολιτεία simply —is described at length in the earlier books of the "Republic"; it is based upon a sort of *caste* system, but one of *worth*, not of *birth*. The finest natures are to be carefully selected and trained from youth upwards, for they are to constitute the highest class in the State—that of Guardians or φύλακες. The rest of the community consists of inferior natures; and in order to get a "sanction" for this necessary submission of the inferior to the superior, Plato tells us that recourse will have to be had to a fable or myth,[1] according to which the φύλακες are earth-born and have gold in their souls, whereas the "lower classes" have souls composed, partly or entirely, of the baser metals. Provision is, of course, made for the promotion of a "golden" soul out of the "silver" class to the "golden," and *vice versa*. In what follows we must not forget that Plato is dealing only with the φύλακες or highest class; the main principle by which the regulations laid down for these is directed is the

The φύλακες.

---

[1] This, of course, though not *literally* true and known as such to the φύλακες, is true *in effect*. We may compare many Christian dogmas, which, because they inspire good *ideals*, we have to present to less intelligent people as though they were true *facts*.

desire that they should have no inducements to neglect the public interests. Hence they must have no private property, for it is material possessions which so readily lead a man's soul away from the pursuit of the highest ideals. They have been chosen with extreme care in infancy, and the greatest importance is attached to their education; a programme of studies is laid down for them; their external life is regulated by the State, they live and have meals in common (Plato much admired the συσσίτια at Sparta), and are brought up—apart from their parents—amid surroundings that will save them from all degrading influences. Thus there is some hope that they will be able to despise the objects of ἐπιθυμία and θυμός, and to attain to the love of wisdom and of beauty, much in the manner described by Diotima in the "Symposium."[1] When they have grown up, the communal mode of living is still maintained. It must be admitted that there are details in the scheme which are repugnant to our modern ideas; the same education is laid down for women as for men, and the scheme involves the abolition of the family and a "community of women and children"—for the best men must be allowed to associate with the best women, and the children must be the children of the State, brought up to serve its best interests apart from the idiosyncracies of their human parents. We are given full details of the military training, and rules for procedure in war, when the women accompany the men as camp-followers.[2] All is planned to lead up to the crowning development—the ideal State under the leadership of the "philosopher-King," in whom political power and the spiri of true science are united, apparently under the convic

[1] Above, p. 85.
[2] This once sounded ridiculous, but cf. our W.A.A.C.

tion that human life will be as nearly ideal as possible if it be regulated by the best possible knowledge on all subjects.

The only practical effort which Plato is said to have made —at the instigation of Dio—to realize this, in the training of Dionysius the younger of Syracuse, ended, as we have mentioned, in complete failure; and in his later dialogue of the "Laws" he made considerable modifications in his ideas (e.g. the abolition of private property and of the family is no longer demanded). But, although never *practically* realized, the ideals of statesmanship which are worked out are, most of them, *theoretically* sound for all time. But we may learn also from facts as well as from theories; so Plato goes on, in the later books of the "Republic," to examine what constitutions have actually been realized in Greece. It is not in any sense an historical survey, but rather a psychological exposition of the traits in human nature that bring about different organizations of society. There is, in fact, a very close connexion between the psychology and the politics of Plato. The three "parts" of the soul correspond to different forms of government or political organization. These which remain to be mentioned are all "perversions," as it were, of the true πολιτεία— Aristotle would call them παρεκβάσεις, παρεκβεβηκυῖαι πολιτεῖαι —expressions of those inferior natures who bulk so largely, though nothing is said of them, in the whole discussion of the φύλακες. The State is nothing but man "writ large," and so we must discuss all these inferior types of men and the different constitutions under which they find their most natural expression. But perhaps it will be well first to set out the correspondence between the politics and the psychology of Plato by the following table. We arrange

Degenerate Polities.

the polities in their logical (not historical) order of degeneration from the ideal polity.[1]

Polity.	Quality of the Soul.
1. Τιμοκρατία	θυμός
2. Ὀλιγαρχία	
3. Δημοκρατία	ἐπιθυμία
4. Τύραννις	

Under oligarchy—which is the "highest" expression of ἐπιθυμία—some sort of order and discipline is maintained; the "appetites" of the many are checked in that they have to submit to the dominion of the few; whereas under democracy they find free play for the unrestrained indulgence of their appetites. The ἐπιθυμία, which is embodied under tyranny, is the ἐπιθυμία of an individual who is suddenly given power to realize it to the full. Δημοκρατία hardly corresponds to what we mean by "democracy" to-day. We are all influenced by the conditions of our age, and Plato's ideas of δημοκρατία were derived from the excessive licence indulged in by the Athenian democracy, or ochlocracy, as it might more rightly be styled, when once the restraining hand of Pericles had been removed.

If we ask how these degenerate polities have arisen, the answer is that they are simply political manifestations of the fact that man is not perfect. In some sense a people has the government which it deserves; and the ideal polity has never been realized in the sphere of practice simply because society does not yet consist of ideal individuals.

[1] Ἀριστοκρατία—the embodiment of ὁμόνοια and λόγος—is omitted from the table, for it is not very clear how it differs from the true πολιτεία in which τὸ λογιστικὸν μέρος finds its expression. "Birth," of course, predominates under aristocracy, but it seems to differ chiefly in that it was practically realized, to some extent, whereas ἡ πολιτεία is purely ideal.

When Plato speaks of the degeneration of such polities from his ideal, he is speaking logically, or philosophically, of the failure to realize his ideal, and not of any actual process of degeneration in time. It comes about because the λογιστικὸν μέρος of the soul has not yet succeeded in doing its proper work of controlling the baser activities of θυμός and ἐπιθυμία; hence στάσις arises, which, as all readers of Greek history know, is a very real factor in the troubles of Greek political life. The "transition" from one polity to another becomes clear if we examine how the "timocratic man" degenerates into the "oligarchic man"; when in the individual the less worthy manifestations of each of the three "parts" of the soul gradually acquire more and more power, until they are the *only* manifestations of that "part"; then that "part" itself degenerates into the one below it, and θυμός, for example, is no longer θυμός but ἐπιθυμία. And as it is with man—the microcosmos—so it is with the macrocosmos of the State.[1]

III. Myths

In the conversation of the uneducated we have all noticed an attempt to eke out their inability to express themselves by appending the word "like" to their statements; "I was all in a muddle, like," and "He was quite done up, like," are undoubtedly the outcome of very vivid impressions in the mind of the speaker, and the "like" is, as it were, an appeal to the hearer to eke out the imperfections of the words with his own thoughts; that very "as it were" is prompted by a diffidence in the possibility of conveying the exact meaning intended through the medium of language. It is the same feeling that prompts the use of the words "so

III. The Myths of Plato.

---

[1] Upon this subject the reader should refer to chapter xiii. of R. L. Nettleship's "Lectures on the Republic of Plato".

to speak" to make a qualification or to soften a strong word. And how often in any argument, at all abstruse, do we not find ourselves, in despair of conveying our meaning in any other way, exclaiming "Let me put it to you in a figure!" This is the function of the myth in Plato; it comes in to expound something which cannot adequately be described in logical argument, something which transcends our ordinary categories of thought (it is expressed in language, of course, but it is picture-language); it is Plato's means of succeeding in the attempt which most of us give up with the exclamation of "I can *feel* it, but I can't *explain* it." Professor Stewart[1] has well expounded this significance of the μῦθος: Plato, he says, "appeals to the major part of man's nature which is not articulate and logical, but feels, and wills, and acts—to that part which cannot explain what a thing is, or how it happens, but feels that a thing is good or bad, and expresses itself, not scientifically in 'existential' or 'theoretic judgments,' but practically in 'value-judgments'—or rather 'value-feelings'. . . . This effect which Plato produces by the Myth in the Dialogue is, it is hardly necessary to say, produced in various degrees by Nature herself, without the aid of literary or other art. The sense of "might, majesty, and dominion" which comes over us as we look into the depths of the starry sky, the sense of our own short time passing, passing, with which we see the lilacs bloom again—these, and many like them, are natural experiences which closely resemble the effect produced in the reader's mind by Plato's art. When these natural moods are experienced, we feel "That which was, and is, and ever shall be" overshadowing

[1] "The Myths of Plato," p. 21.

us; and familiar things—the stars, and the lilac bloom—become suddenly strange and wonderful, for our eyes are opened to see that they declare its presence. It is such moods of feeling in his cultivated reader that Plato induces, satisfies, and regulates by Myths which set forth God, Soul, and Cosmos in vision." We think at once of "the light that never was on sea or land," and Profesor Stewart goes on to point out that the effect produced upon us by the myth—this "transcendental feeling"—is essentially that of poetry. "The conclusion which follows, as it seems to me, from examination of what one experiences in perusing great Poetry, ... is that the essential charm of Poetry—that for the sake of which, in the last resort, it exists—lies in its power of inducing, in certain carefully chosen circumstances, that mode of Transcendental Feeling which is experienced as a solemn sense of the over-shadowing presence of "That which was, and is, and ever shall be." The Poet, always by means of Representations—images, μιμήματα—products of the dream-consciousness in himself, and often with the aid of Rhythm and Melody, which call up certain shadowy Feelings, strange, in their shadowy form, to ordinary consciousness, induces in his patient the dream-consciousness in which such Representations and Feelings are at home.... It is at the moment of waking from one of these lapses into the dream-world that the solemn sense of the immediate presence of "That which was, and is, and ever shall be" is experienced—at the moment when one sees, in the world of wide-awake consciousness, the image, or hears the melody, which one saw or heard only a moment ago—or was it not ages ago?—in the dream-world."[1]

[1] "The Myths of Plato," p. 33.

It is by means of the μῦθος that Plato sets forth his inmost convictions about the soul and immortality; in the "Phædo," for example, with its doctrine of σῶμα σῆμα —that the body is a tomb within which the soul is "cabined, cribb'd, confined, bound in" during its appearance on earth, clogged and impeded by all the material limitations of the corporeal,—the "intellectual" arguments for its immortality are clinched, as it were, by the myth with which the dialogue closes. In the "Phædrus" the soul is described as that which moves itself (τὸ αὐτὸ ἑαυτὸ κινοῦν), and its immortality can be "intellectually" deduced from this definition; for that which has "mechanical" motion, as we say, which is impelled by some other thing, and itself imparts motion to a third thing, may be conceived of as ceasing to move; but that which moves itself can never cease to move, for it is the source of motion (ἀρχὴ κινήσεως).[1] Such a source of motion can never have come into being, for everything that comes into being has had a beginning, but the soul is itself the beginning (ἀρχή) of motion. Similarly, it can never come to an end, for, if it ceased to be, then everything in the world would cease moving. Therefore the soul is immortal. But such a proof leaves us rather cold; and so we are made to *feel* the immortality of the soul in the myth which follows, wherein it is likened unto a charioteer driving two winged horses. The myths usually come at the end of the dialogues, for the simple reason that their function commences where that of ἐπιστήμη ends; when all that intellectual argument can do has been done,

[1] Thus, at last, is motion explained, after it has troubled the history of philosophy for so long. It is found to be a spiritual thing; no wonder, then, that it evaded all the efforts of the earlier materialistic speculations to account for it.

then the myth comes in to make us *feel* what we have been attempting to *think;* feeling—as so often with Plato—comes in as a sort of guarantee of the rightness of thought. The discourse of Diotima in the "Symposium," of which the conclusion has already been quoted, is of the nature of a myth; and we have also referred to the brief indication of the μῦθος in the "Republic" by which it is sought to sanction the régime of the φύλακες. The most famous of all is the myth of Er with which the "Republic" closes. Er is supposed to have been killed in battle, but, having come to life again when laid on the funeral pyre, he describes how his soul journeyed to the celestial region, where he saw judgment given upon the different souls of men according to the lives which they had led on earth. In course of time they are summoned together to make fresh choice of lives, according as each would wish to be in his second appearance upon earth. They appear before the thrones of the Fates—those daughters of Necessity, Lachesis, Clotho, and Atropos—marshalled by a prophet who, taking lots from the lap of Lachesis together with ensamples of different lives, bids the souls cast lots for the order of their choosing and then choose, of their own free will, the kind of life which they would like—αἰτία ἑλομένου · θεὸς ἀναίτιος. The "ensamples" are of all kinds—tyrannies; fame as an athlete or for personal beauty; wealth and poverty; health and disease—and most of the souls choose a life as different as possible from that which they experienced in their previous appearance upon earth. Thus Plato, while incidentally animadverting upon the insubstantiality of the commonly received opinions about human happiness, is really dealing with the great problem of "free will"—a problem about which more conviction may be gained by the adumbrations

The Myth of Er.

of a myth than from the most reasoned of dialectical arguments.

Most of the myths are, unfortunately, rather too long for quotatation in this book, but they have been collected, translated, and expounded by Prof. J. A. Stewart in his " Myths of Plato," to which we must refer the reader. But in order to give some idea of their nature we append one of the shorter ones. It is the myth from the " Protagoras " which deals with such things as the συνοικισμός of the πόλις and with what constitutes the difference between man and the beasts and makes for his kinship with the gods.

The Protagoras Myth.
There was once a time when there were gods, but no race of mortals. Now when the destined time came for these too to be created, the gods fashioned them in the centre of the earth, with a mixture of earth and fire and all the things which fire and earth blend into. And when they were ready to lead them up to the light, they ordered Prometheus and Epimetheus to furnish and distribute to each suitable powers. Epimetheus begged Prometheus to let him make the distribution. "When I have distributed them," said he, "you inspect them." So when he had persuaded him thus, he made the distribution. And in the distribution he endowed some with strength without speed, and those that were weaker he furnished with speed: to some he gave arms, and for those that were unarmed he contrived some other power which would keep them safe: to those which he clothed in small bodies, he assigned winged flight or a retreat under the earth: those which he made large were to be saved by their very size: and so with other things he made an equal distribution. He devised things thus so that no one species should disappear. Then when he had provided for them a means of escape from each other's slaughter, he contrived to give them comfort against the seasons sent by Zeus, by clothing them in thick fur and tough skins, suitable for keeping out the cold and the heat, and which, when they sought sleep, would furnish for them their own natural bed: under the feet to some he gave hoofs, to others hair and tough bloodless skin. Next he provided different nourishment for each, for some the herbs of the earth, for others the fruits of trees, for others roots: and some there were whose food was other animals. But these he afflicted with barrenness in birth; to their prey he gave fecundity, as a safeguard for the

IDEALISTIC INTERPRETATION OF UNIVERSE

species. Now, because Epimetheus was not altogether wise, he expended all his gifts on the brutes without noticing it: and there still remained the race of men unprovided for, wherefore he was at a loss what to do. While he was thus in doubt Prometheus came to him to inspect the distribution, and saw that all the other animals were carefully provided for, but that man was naked and unshod, without bed or arms. Yet the destined day was already at hand, on which man too had to go from the earth into the light. Thus while Prometheus was still at a loss what safeguard to find for man, he stole the cunning craft of Athene and Hephæstus, and with it fire, for without fire it was impossible either to acquire or use it, and these gifts he gave to man. Thus it was that man obtained the crafts of life, but the art of politics he had not: for Zeus kept this. Now into the citadel, the house of Zeus, Prometheus was not yet allowed to enter; besides, the guards of Zeus were indeed terrible. But into the common house of Athene and Hephæstus, while they were occupied with their favourite craft, he crept unnoticed, and stealing the fiery craft of Hephæstus and that of Athene he gave them to man. Hence man obtained plenteous resources for life, but Prometheus, it is said, through the forgetfulness of Epimetheus, not long after payed the penalty of his theft. Thus since man had a portion with the gods, because of this relationship with them, he was in the first place the only one among the animals who worshipped gods and attempted to raise to them altars and images: next by means of his art he fashioned sounds and words, and found for himself habitations, and clothes, and footwear, and beds, and nourishment from the earth. Thus provided for, men in the beginning lived scattered apart, and cities there were none. Therefore they were destroyed by the wild beasts, because on every side they were weaker than they, and, though their craftsmanship was sufficient aid to them for self-support, it was insufficient for waging war against the wild beasts. For they had not the art of politics, of which the art of waging war is a part. Therefore they sought to gather together and to find safety by building cities, but when they were gathered together they wronged each other, because they had not the art of politics, and again they scattered and began to perish. Then Zeus, fearing for our race lest it should wholly perish, sent Hermes carrying reverence and justice to men, that they might bring order to the cities and be links binding men together in friendship. So Hermes asked Zeus in what manner he should give reverence and justice to men. "As the crafts were distributed to them," said he, "shall I so distribute these? For they were assigned in this manner: One man was given the art of medicine, and he sufficed for many others, and so with the rest of the crafts. Shall I then give reverence and justice to men in like manner, or shall I distribute them to all?"—"To all," answered Zeus: "let all have a share. For otherwise cities could not exist, if as with the crafts only a few had a share. Further, lay down this law from me, that he who cannot share in reverence and justice is to be killed as a pest to the city." This is the reason then, Socrates, why the Athenians and others, whenever skill in carpentry or any other handicraft is in question, think that only a few are capable of advising, and if any other than these few gives advice they will not listen to him as you say: and in my opinion it is quite natural. But when they come to deliberate upon political virtue, which depends entirely upon justice and moderation, they listen quite rightly to any man, deeming that it befits every man to share in this virtue without which there can be no cities. This, Socrates, is the true cause of this fact (320c8-323a3).

Epistemology. In dealing with a writer like Plato, especially when one has in view readers such as those for whom this book is primarily intended, one must be eclectic, but one must try to preserve something like a due balance in the exposition of so many-sided an author. Nevertheless, most of the later "intellectual" dialogues are quite unsuited for school reading, though they are, in some respects, Plato's greatest contribution to philosophy. They set forth the later developments of his epistemology, or science of knowledge, which is far too important to be entirely omitted here. But in order to make a difficult subject more easy to follow we will, before dealing with our fourth, and last, aspect of Platonic doctrine, make a brief survey of the development of philosophical speculation, especially with reference to its bearing upon epistemology, from the earliest times of Thales up to the point at which Plato takes up the development. We shall thus be more readily able to understand the significance of his contribution.

We saw at the beginning of this book how the first attitude of man towards the external universe is what we have called a *theological interpretation* of things. It might equally well be called *mythological*, for it is largely the product of imagination, and is really prior to anything that can rightly be called philosophy. It is soon felt to be inadequate; for, in so far as it is an explanation of things at all, it is an explanation in terms of another world from this in which we live. Man wants an explanation of his everyday world, of the things which he can touch and see; and so we get as our first philosophical speculation a frank materialism, as seen in the early Ionian philosophers. The difficulty of materialism is that it cannot explain motion; the ἔκκρισις of "the pairs" in Anaximander, the πύκνωσις and ἀραίωσις of Anaximenes, are really tacit admissions of this difficulty. In Heraclitus motion, though still unexplained, is everywhere—πάντα ῥεῖ. This constitutes a complete breakdown of materialistic monism; and we see in Pythagoras and Xenophanes philosophy no longer confining itself to τὸ τῆς ὕλης εἶδος. Incidentally, it is Xenophanes who gives us the first really philosophical speculations upon theology—he objects alike to anthropomorphism and to polytheism; and it is in him that the *idea of unity* first becomes prominent. The continual flux of phenomena, according to the πάντα ῥεῖ theory, is such that it becomes quite impossible to predicate anything about them; the very possibility of knowledge slips from our grasp. But we do know something about the world; there is a certain permanence and stability both in our knowledge and in things. Eleatic monism stresses this unity to the extent of denying the reality of motion, which it cannot explain on materialistic suppositions. It is a unity, however, which belongs rather to the sphere of τὸ τί ἦν εἶναι than to that of ὕλη; but there is still an attempt to find an explanation within this sphere though philosophy by no means confines itself thereto. Both

Empedocles and Anaxagoras, the one with his Love and Strife, and the other with his νοῦς, bring into prominence what lay hid more or less in Anaximander and Anaximenes. But materialistic monism is hopeless; so we get a materialistic pluralism in the atoms of Leucippus and Democritus, by whom what is reality is explained as something so entirely different from our sense-presentations that we are driven to reflect upon the nature of our sense-perception. Up to this point the external world had been taken, as it were, *de facto* for granted, as being such as it is presented to us in sense-perception. But with the stage of reflection, to which Eleaticism on the one hand and atomism on the other, have driven us, we get a very clear distinction between *sense-perception* and *thought*; henceforth epistemology becomes the main concern of philosophy.[1] It is realized that in my attempt to learn about the world I am, in some sense, confined to the sphere of my own ideas. On what grounds can I say that these ideas represent reality? What about illusion and fallacy? Of the two faculties of sense-perception and thought the latter is accepted as somehow the higher and less fallible faculty; hence comes a period of dialectical or eristic play of thought, without any consideration of the truth, or otherwise, of the *data* supplied by the senses. This is the age of the Sophists, of Protagoras with his πάντων μέτρον ἄνθρωπος. Now in order to get over such extreme subjectivism we must examine thought and see what claim it has to represent reality.

When I reflect upon the phenomenal world presented to me

---

[1] This is somewhat obscured by the predominately ethical interests of Socrates, so that the *theory of conduct*, which is more interesting to the average man than is epistemology, occupies the foreground for some time; but philosophy returns inevitably to its natural development in Plato.

by my senses, I cannot believe that it exists *by* my perception, though it may exist *for* my senses. I am willing to relinquish any idea I may ever have had of a reality apart from my perception of it; but this does not imply that it exists *because* I see it. The function of thought is to interpret what I see, and neither to establish reality in a world beyond phenomena, nor to dissolve it in the subjective affections of my own brain. It must enable us to decide what phenomena are illusion and what are not, but it is among phenomena that it must find reality. *Reality is the world of phenomena better understood, not another world beyond them.* By this process of thought I gradually get built up a well-ordered system, which hangs together because it is consistent. There is thus a "unity amid diversity," and the solution of the predication troubles of earlier philosophy in the recognition that ἐστίν does not denote identity, but represents in language this act of thought, this reference to reality, this ordering of the vague presentations of sense. The Sophists had played fast and loose with the discovery of the paramount importance of thought; it is Socrates first, and then Plato, who bring us back to sober sense by showing us the real function of thought in building up our knowledge, in finding the ἓν εἶδος amongst the diversity of sense-presentations.[1]

IV. The Ideas

The Platonic doctrine of ideas may be briefly stated as follows. In the sense-perception of phenomena what I see is one particular instance, as it were, of a thing. Such a particular is a representation (μίμημα) of the universal or

[1] This survey has necessarily become metaphysical; but, even if not fully understood, it should help the reader to grasp the significance of the Platonic "ideas," to which we now direct his attention.

"idea" (ἰδέα, εἶδος). Thus any individual chair, for example, conforms to the general shape and design of the "idea of a chair," to that visionary pattern which makes it more suitable for sitting on than for packing books in; or—an example from the moral sphere—any act of bravery is a specific action, performed by an individual, in this place, and at this time, but the quality which it exhibits passes beyond chronological and geographical limitations; it is a general idea, a universal notion, of which my particular act of bravery is but one manifestation, here and now, one case out of many acts of bravery. The relation between the particular and the universal, between phenomena and the ideas, is variously expressed by Plato. At one time phenomena are said to be representations (μιμήματα) which "participate in" (μετέχει) the idea; at other times the idea is said "to be present in" (παρεῖναι) the particular, and it is also spoken of as the archetype (παράδειγμα) of which the particular is a copy.[1] We must make allowances for the difficulty of expressing a new philosophical conception in language, especially in language which has not yet developed a technical phraseology. But there can be no doubt that the Platonic "idea" corresponds, in many of its aspects, to what is called, in modern logic, the *concept* or *notion*. Looked at from one point of view, such a concept is gained by abstraction from concrete particulars; but from another point of view this is not so. Plato's ἰδέαι are said to exist apart from, and prior to, all concrete embodiment. It is because the soul already knows the archetype that it can recognize it in a concrete particular. Hence we see the connexion between the doctrine of ideas and the doctrine that all know-

---

[1] Prof. Jackson maintains that these are not different ways of speaking of the same thing, and sees a development in Plato from an earlier, mimetic, to a later (paradeigmatic) theory of ideas.

ledge is recollection (ἀνάμνησις). Let us examine this doctrine. It springs from the old Pythagorean belief in παλιγγενεσία and is associated in Plato both with the pre-existence of the soul and with its survival after death. But there are two possible meanings of ἀνάμνησις which it is im-portant to distinguish. That "knowledge is recollection" may mean that I know a particular thing because I saw that particular thing in my previous existence and now remember it, much as Pythagoras recognized the shield of Euphorbus in the temple where he had dedicated it. In other words, I "recollect" knowledge which I had acquired in my pre-existence through the ordinary human channel of αἴσθησις of phenomena; my portion of the waters of Lethe, that is to say, has not been permanently effective. The reader will notice that such an interpretation as this of the ἀνάμνησις doctrine is no contribution to the theory of knowledge at all; it only explains my knowledge now by referring it back to a previous, entirely similar, and unexplained knowledge on a different occasion. But Plato obviously did mean it as a part of his theory of knowledge. The second possible meaning of "recollection," and undoubtedly the one intended, and indeed specifically described, by Plato, is that in the spirit world, as it were, the soul has seen the archetypes of things, and thus, when it enters into the human body it is able to recognize the things of which it has previously known those archetypes. It is thus that Plato expresses symbolically that aspect of the "ideas" in which they cannot be said to be derived by generalization from concrete particulars. The mind is such as to be able to comprehend ideas, or, as Aristotle would say, they exist in it potentially (δυνάμει) though not actually (ἐνεργείᾳ). It is in this sense that the Platonic "ideas" are said to exist apart from any particular mani-

[margin: ἀνάμνησις.]

festation of them. As we have already seen, in the simplest act of perception there is an element contributed by the subjective side, by the perceiving subject; and in the act of knowledge there is an "interpretation" of what is presented by the senses.¹ Similarly with the "ideas" of the moral virtues; we may be said to know them when we "interpret" them correctly and can see them in all their bearings, refer them to their correct places in the system, giving them their right values in relation to the whole of human conduct. As Prof. Stewart says, "to find the εἴδη of the moral virtues" is "to *explain* the moral virtues by exhibiting each in its special context—by assigning to each its special place and use in the social system. . . . 'Context grasped,' 'scientific point of view taken,' 'εἶδος discovered' —these are equivalent expressions.".²

There is another aspect of the Platonic ideas—what Prof. Stewart calls their "æsthetic" aspect—in which the εἶδος appears as an object of rapt contemplation when we are brought face to face with the very Presence of Beauty. Compare what was said above about the love of beauty in the quotation from the "Symposium," and that "transcendental feeling" to which the μῦθος appeals. But it would only confuse the issue to describe this aspect at length here.³

This doctrine of ideas will be seen to contain a solution of the previous difficulties about the One and the Many, and gives a clear and intelligible meaning to that "unity amid diversity" which we have mentioned before. It is Plato's great contribution to the theory of knowledge and plays a prominent part in the metaphysical speculations of his later "critical" or "intellectual" dialogues, such as the "Par-

---

¹ See above, p. 52.   ² Plato's "Doctrine of Ideas," p. 7.
³ Cf. also the "contemplation" of *instances* above, p. 82.

menides," "Theætetus," and "Sophistes." These things are too abstract for detailed treatment here, but we will conclude with a brief indication of the matters treated in one of them. The "Theætetus" is an examination of the nature of knowledge (ἐπιστήμη), first, of the proposition that it is equivalent to αἴσθησις—a proposition which is identified with the Protagorean maxim of πάντων μέτρον ἄνθρωπος; man is the measure of all things; things are what they seem to me to be; ἐπιστήμη = αἴσθησις. But this is obviously not so, for, as we have seen above, there is an element contributed by the mind in the simplest act of sense-perception; all sensation is a relation of the external object and the percipient subject, a combination of agent and patient. Then the very fact that we can compare different sensations one with another implies that there is within us some higher principle which is able to do so, for such comparison involves the bringing of the various sensations before a higher court, as it were; and so Theætetus proposes the second definition that knowledge is right opinion (ὀρθὴ δόξα). We perceive not *by* our senses, but *through* them; perceptions enter by these channels and pass to the common sense or centre of life (εἰς μίαν τινὰ ἰδέαν πάντα ταῦτα συντείνει) and so the mind passes judgment upon them. If it judges correctly, then we have knowledge; ἐπιστήμη = ὀρθὴ δόξα. But we can have true judgment without knowledge. Think of the law-courts, for example, where an eloquent and persuasive pleader may succeed in inducing the jury to come to a true judgment by the mere force of his rhetoric without detailing the true significance of the facts which justify such a judgment. This leads to the third definition of knowledge as being right judgment supported by a proper reason (ἀληθὴς δόξα μετὰ λόγου). The superiority of this third definition over the second obviously depends entirely upon the meaning attached to the μετὰ λόγου. Does this only amount to a "judgment" about the trueness of the opinion? If so, it does not help at all, for we have decided that "judgment" is no criterion of truth. If, on the other hand, the λόγος *is* knowledge, then we are arguing in a circle. With this the dialogue ends, without, as is so frequent with Plato, a definite answer being given to all the difficulties raised; but it has taught us that ἐπιστήμη is neither sensation nor the independent activity of the mind.

CHAPTER VI

ARISTOTLE AND THE TELEOLOGICAL CONCEPTION OF THE UNIVERSE

ARISTOTLE (384-322 B.C.) was not an Athenian by birth, having been born at Stagira, a Greek colony in Thrace. But he came to Athens when barely an ἔφηβος, and studied under Plato for nearly twenty years. Upon the latter's death in 347 B.C. he left Athens, and subsequently became, at the request of Philip of Macedon, tutor to his young son Alexander, the boy who was to become famous as Alexander the Great. When Alexander set out upon his great Persian expedition in 335 B.C., Aristotle returned to Athens, where he taught, until shortly before his death, at the Lyceum. *Life.*

There could scarcely be a greater difference of style than that which exists between Plato and Aristotle, the one almost a philosophical dreamer, the other a "hard intellectualist." Plato's human interest is, as we have remarked, indicated by the very form of his writings—that of the dialogue, peopled, as it always is with him, by very real and often by very lovable *personæ*. In the words of a great admirer of this aspect of him:[1] "If Plato did not create the 'Socrates' of his 'Dialogues,' he has created other characters hardly less life-like. The young Charmides, the incarnation of natural, as the aged Cephalus of acquired temperance; his Sophoclean *Contrasted with Plato.*

---

[1] Walter Pater in his "Plato and Platonism," p. 129.

amenity as he sits there pontifically at the altar, in the court of his peaceful house; the large company, of varied character and of every age, which moves in those 'Dialogues,' though still oftenest the young in all their youthful liveliness—who that knows them at all can doubt Plato's hold on persons, that of persons on him? Sometimes, even when they are not formally introduced into his work, characters that had interested, impressed, or touched him, inform and colour it, as if with their personal influence, showing through what purports to be the wholly abstract analysis of some wholly abstract moral situation." There is nothing of this sort in Aristotle, who did not favour the dialogue form. His teaching is set forth in a series of reasoned treatises, of set "hand-books" upon ethics, politics, or metaphysics.¹

I. *The Ethics of Aristotle.*—One of the most prominent features of Aristotelian doctrine is the conception of τὸ τέλος,

¹ Not only is Aristotle's philosophy expounded in a series of set treatises, but it is often put in very technical language. As instances of this we may adduce :—

1. κατὰ συμβεβηκός, or *accidental* : this is opposed to καθ' αὐτό ; for example, if a man who is a musician builds a house, then he does so κατὰ συμβεβηκός, he need not necessarily, or indeed usually, do so. Similarly a sculptor, for example, may be "accidentally" bald.

2. ἀναγκαῖον ἐξ ὑποθέσεως, or *hypothetically necessary*, i.e. a prerequisite for something else desired ; a *sine qua non*, or, as Aristotle himself defines it, ὧν ἄνευ τὸ ἀγαθὸν μὴ ἐνδέχεται ἢ εἶναι ἢ γενέσθαι, e.g. if an ailing man wants to get well it is ἀναγκαῖον ἐξ ὑποθέσεως to take medicine, though taking medicine is no necessary part of health.

3. δυνάμει (*potentially*) is opposed to ἐνεργείᾳ (*actually*). A child is potentially an adult, because it has the power (δύναμις) of developing into one. Similarly a man who knows how to play the harp is ἐνεργείᾳ a harp-player only when doing so.

4. πρότερον τῇ φύσει, or *logically prior*. The whole is logically prior to its parts, though it may not be prior in time. In taking a railway-journey my destination is logically prior to my departure from home.

TELEOLOGICAL CONCEPTION OF UNIVERSE 115

of a purpose in things, whether they be the most insignificant of artificial products or the highest manifestations of man's activity. This "teleological" conception, as we call it, applies not only to man, but also to Nature herself; for who τὸ τέλος. that considers the wonderful articulation of a flower or of a plant can imagine that such structures have come into being purposelessly, by chance, as it were, and without design? No, there is ordered purpose, a meaning and an object in all that Nature does: ἡ δὲ φύσις ἀεὶ ζητεῖ τέλος, he says in the "De Generatione Animalium." The opening words of his treatise on "Ethics" are πᾶσα τέχνη καὶ πᾶσα μέθοδος, ὁμοίως δὲ πρᾶξίς τε καὶ προαίρεσις, ἀγαθοῦ τινὸς ἐφίεσθαι δοκεῖ—"every art and every investigation, as likewise every action and moral purpose, is believed to aim at some good." It is the τέλος that reveals the real significance of a thing (compare the importance attached in a modern law-court to determining the *motive* of a crime); it is that by which it can most readily be defined, ὁρίζεται γὰρ ἕκαστον τῷ τέλει ("Ethics," 1115b, 22). We may begin, then, our investigation into the aim of human life with the admitted principle that the good is that which all things seek (οὗ πάντ' ἐφίεται, "Ethics," 1094a, 3). Everyone desires what he thinks good; but different things appear good to different people. A man's conception of "the good" varies in accordance with the kind of life which he leads. Now there are three kinds of life:—

1. ὁ ἀπολαυστικὸς βίος
2. ὁ πολιτικὸς βίος
3. ὁ θεωρητικὸς βίος

The three Lives.

To the man who leads the life of pleasure (ὁ ἀπολαυστικὸς βίος) pleasure (ἡδονή) seems to be the chief good; to him who lives the πολιτικὸς βίος, takes part in the government of his city, and contends for "offices" in competition with his fellow-men, honour (τιμή) or worthiness (ἀρετή) seems to be the chief good, much as it is to-day for the man whose ideal in life is to become a town-councillor, or mayor of his city. But the aim of the highest or θεωρητικὸς βίος—the life of speculation—is εὐδαιμονία, a term which it will be our business to explain later. We can see at once, however, that τιμή will not do as a conception of "the good," for we desire to be honoured not for *anything* or by *anyone*, but by discerning people (οἱ φρόνιμοι), and for our good qualities (ἐπ' ἀρετῇ). It is no pleasure to me to be respected by small boys, because I carry a "swagger" cane, or have a fine, silken moustache. And there is a further objection to taking τιμή as "the good," for it seems to belong rather to the person who honours than to the person honoured (δοκεῖ γὰρ ἐν τοῖς τιμῶσι μᾶλλον εἶναι ἢ ἐν τῷ τιμωμένῳ, "Ethics," 1095b, 25); whereas my "good" must be something which is essentially mine, something which no one can take from me (οἰκεῖόν τι καὶ δυσαφαίρετον).[1] Nor can it be ἀρετή, for a good man may meet with great misfortune, or he may be virtuous and yet inactive or asleep all his life. Now we must make our inquiry in a practical way, and avoid all such highly abstract conceptions as the Platonic ἰδέα τἀγαθοῦ; we may be able to make our way up to some general principle, but we must start from palpable facts and proceed inductively (ἐπὶ τὰς ἀρχάς). The "good" of every art and of everything else is οὗ χάριν τὰ λοιπὰ πράττεται, i.e. τὸ τέλος, so that if there is any τέλος of all that

marginalia: εὐδαιμονία, not τιμή, nor ἀρετή.

---

[1] The idea is the same as that which made Socrates (see above, p. 67) say that no evil can befall a good man so long as he remains such. The human "good" is a disposition of the soul, which renders a man happy, no matter what adventitious circumstances may do. Cf. Henley's "I am the captain of my soul," and Epictetus *passim*. Aristotle's doctrine is, however, a modification upon the extreme idealism of Socrates, as appears in the remark immediately following about ἀρετή.

man does, of all πρακτά, this will be τὸ πρακτὸν ἀγαθόν, as was said before. All τέλη are not the same in kind; some, for example, are subordinate to others, mere ὄργανα, such as flutes or wealth. The τέλος of the art of the flute-*maker* is "flutes," but these are mere instruments of happiness in the hands of the flute-*player;* wealth, though pursued by many people as though it were an end in life, is merely a means to enjoyment, and—as indeed we often, or rather, always, see in the case of those who do not realize that it is a mere means—may conceivably fail to bring what we desire. Our "good" must be no such means; it must be final and complete in itself (τέλειον), something which is chosen for its own sake. This is, somewhat dogmatically, here stated to be εὐδαιμονία, which is self-sufficing (αὐταρκής) and is something which cannot be equated with other "goods" (μὴ συναριθμουμένη); and such a quality is necessary in the final good which we are seeking, for otherwise the least addition of any other good thing would make it more desirable, so that it would no longer, in itself, be οὗ πάντ' ἐφίεται. But before we can fully comprehend the nature of εὐδαιμονία we must make a long investigation with the object of obtaining a more precise definition of it. Now the "good" of a thing always lies in its function,[1] and so we may begin by asking "What is the function of man?" It is not simply life, for that he shares with the vegetable kingdom; nor is it conscious or percipient life, for that is common to all animals; but man is a rational being, an active agent, and so we may define his function as "an activity of the soul in accordance with reason" (ψυχῆς ἐνέργεια κατὰ λόγον). Man's life is the highest type of the three:—

The "Good" defined by the Function.

1. ἡ θρεπτικὴ καὶ αὐξητικὴ ζωή (common to man and plants).

---

[1] A principle which Aristotle owed to his biological studies.

2. ἡ αἰσθητικὴ ζωή (common to all animals).

3. (ζωή) πρακτική τις τοῦ λόγον ἔχοντος (peculiar to man).

Preliminary Definition. But the function of a thing is done well when it is done in accordance with the proper excellence (κατὰ τὴν οἰκείαν ἀρετήν) of that thing. Hence we can define man's good as ψυχῆς ἐνέργεια κατ' ἀρετήν. Perhaps we should add ἐν βίῳ τελείῳ, for a man must live a reasonable length of time in order to "realize himself," as we say, and he must be adequately supplied with the χορηγία of virtue.

As this is one of the most important portions of Aristotle's ethical doctrine we will quote what he says:—

> Now perhaps to call "the Good" εὐδαιμονία seems one of those points upon which all would agree, but its nature needs defining a little more clearly. We might do this by defining the function of man. For as with the flute player and with the sculptor and with every artist—and indeed with all who have functions and are concerned with action—it is admitted that the good and excellence of a thing rests in the work done, so it would seem to be with man, if he has any particular function. Now are there particular functions and actions of a carpenter and a shoemaker, and yet none of man, but he is by nature function-less? Or, just as the eye, and the hand, and the foot, and every member of the body generally has its peculiar function, so is there a definite function beyond all these which one could ascribe to man? What then can this be? "Life" appears common to plants [as well as to man], and we are in search of a function peculiar to man. We must therefore dismiss the life of nourishment and growth. Next would be percipient life, which also seems common to horses and oxen and all animals. There is left a life consisting in the action of the rational part. This part is twofold—as obeying reason, and as possessing and exercising reason. And, as there are two possible ways of "possessing and exercising reason,"[1] we must take for our definition the active sense, for this seems the highest sense. So if the function of man is an activity of the soul according to reason, or not without reason,[2] and if we say that the

---

[1] I.e., as a *state* and as a *function*.

[2] κατὰ λόγον seems to mean under the control of an inward reason actually residing in the individual, while μὴ ἄνευ λόγου means in obedience to the dictates of an external reason.

function of the class and of the good individual is the same—as with "harp-player" and "good harp-player" and so with all other cases, adding excellence to the function; for the function of a harp-player is to play the harp, that of a good harp-player to do so well—if this is the case, then it follows that the "good" of man is an activity of the soul in accordance with his virtue.[1] If man has many virtues, then in accordance with the highest. We must add "in a complete life," for one swallow does not make spring, nor does one day. Similarly a single day or a short space of time cannot make a man blessed and happy. ("Ethics," 1097b22-1098a20).

Let us now proceed to examine our tentative definition in the light of commonly accepted opinions, and see whether it is in agreement with them or not. "Goods" are generally divided into three classes:—

1. τὰ ἐκτὸς ἀγαθά—external goods, such as wealth.
2. τὰ περὶ σῶμα—bodily goods, such as health.
3. τὰ περὶ ψυχήν—spiritual goods.

Three Classes of "Goods".

Of these, the first are provided for by the inclusion of the words ἐν βίῳ τελείῳ in our definition; the third class are generally admitted to be superior to the second, and so we may say that our definition accords with commonly-received opinion. There is no need for us to add "pleasure" to it, externally superimposed, hung round its neck, as it were, (ὥσπερ περίαπτόν τι) for actions which give expression to ourselves, in which we "realize" ourselves, as we say (πράξεις κατὰ τὴν οἰκείαν ἀρετήν), are naturally (φύσει) pleasant. Nor is there any necessity to include "good fortune," for adventitious circumstances (τυχαί) are only ancillary elements, not determining factors of happiness. Just as Socrates held that no evil could befall a good man, so Aristotle regards his εὐδαιμονία as something stable and permanent (μόνιμόν τι καὶ μηδαμῶς εὐμετάβολον), which depends upon the activities of

[1] ἀρετή, of course, is "virtue" in the old English sense of peculiar power or faculty, without the modern *moral* connotation, as we speak of the *virtues* of a herb.

our soul (κύριαι δ' εἰσὶν αἱ κατ' ἀρετὴν ἐνέργειαι τῆς εὐδαιμονίας, "Ethics," 1100b, 10), and cannot be brought about by adventitious circumstances. He admits, however, that we cannot do without favourable circumstances (ἀλλὰ προσδεῖται τούτων [sc. τυχῶν] ὁ ἀνθρώπινος βίος). Small misfortunes will have little or no effect upon us; but a big one will have, because it impedes our activities (ἐμποδίζει πολλαῖς ἐνεργείαις). But, even so, there is a certain moral grandeur in a man's "bearing up," as we say, under adversity; his true worth shines out even in such circumstances (διαλάμπει τὸ καλόν) for the εὐδαίμων is no chameleon-like person (ποικίλος καὶ εὐμετάβολος), taking his character from external τυχαί.

The Moral Virtues. At the commencement of the second book of his "Ethics" Aristotle begins his account of the moral virtues (ἠθικαὶ ἀρεταί) and asks whether they are implanted in us by nature or whether they are acquired. The answer is that they are acquired, for that which exists φύσει cannot be changed by habituation and training (ἐθισμός). Nature gives us the capacity for acquiring them, and this capacity is developed by training. As proof that there are no innate ἀρεταί we have only to consider the difference between the moral virtues and those things which we do possess φύσει. In such cases, the faculties of sight and hearing for example, we have the faculty (δύναμις) first and exhibit the ἐνέργειαι later; no one sees or hears before he has eyes or ears. But we acquire virtue by *doing* virtuous deeds; the virtuous condition (ἕξις) is produced in us by our actions; according as our actions are, such does our character become

Character Determined by Actions. (ἐκ τῶν ὁμοίων ἐνεργειῶν αἱ ἕξεις γίνονται, "Ethics," 1103b, 21); a man *is* what he *does*. If our actions [1] (πράξεις), then, determine

[1] Not every action is, of course, a πρᾶξις or moral act. Putting on my boots in the morning is an action, but it is not a πρᾶξις; it has no

our characters, it is important to define what these should be. We may say two things about them: (1) They should observe the mean (κατὰ τὸν ὀρθὸν λόγον)—compare the modern precept, "moderation in all things"—for excess and defect are alike bad; the μεσότης is good. (2) They are in a way both cause and effect of the ἕξις, e.g. by being temperate we can abstain from pleasures, and by abstaining from pleasures we become temperate; by taking much nourishment we can endure toil, and by enduring toil we become strong. The test of the formation of a ἕξις rests in the pleasure, or pain, accompanying the act. If a man is happy in abstaining from bodily pleasure, then he is σώφρων; but, if miserable, he is ἀκόλαστος. Consequently, as Plato said, a man should be trained from youth to find his pleasures and pains in the right objects (χαίρειν τε καὶ λυπεῖσθαι οἷς ᾿δεῖ), and he must choose those objects of deliberate purpose (προαίρεσις). There is no moral value in a good act done accidentally: it must be intentional (ἐκ προαιρέσεως). Combining these two characteristics—that it must be intended and that it must avoid extremes—we get a definition of moral virtue as ἕξις προαιρετικὴ ἐν μεσότητι οὖσα. This is what is meant when we say that Aristotle regarded the moral virtues as means between two extremes. Consider the following table. Sometimes the abstract quality is given, and sometimes the person who exhibits the quality. It has been thought well to retain Aristotle's exact words, even when there is in Greek an abstract noun for the adjective he used.

Virtue a Mean.

moral significance and does not help to determine my character; it is a momentary action without any permanency of value. Moral actions, on the contrary, are not over and done with as soon as completed; in fact, their significance begins upon their completion, or—to put it grammatically—they belong to the Perfect and not to the Aorist tense.

122 THE ELEMENTS OF GREEK PHILOSOPHY

ὑπερβολή	μεσότης	ἔλλειψις	Sphere Within Which the ἕξις is Exhibited i.e. περί	
δειλός	ἀνδρεία	—	τὸ φοβεῖσθαι	⎫ These ἕξεις can be regarded from two different points of view; the sphere with which they are concerned is a double one. Excess of fear and deficit of confidence are the same, but not excess of confidence and defect of fear.†
θρασύς	—	δειλός	τὸ θαρρεῖν	⎭
ἀκολασία	σωφροσύνη	ἀναισθητοι	ἡδονὰς καὶ λύπας	
* ἀσωτία (*prodigality*)	ἐλευθεριότης	ἀνελευθερία	δόσιν χρημάτων καὶ λῆψιν	
ἀπειροκαλία [or βαναυσία] (*vulgarity*)	μεγαλοπρέπεια	μικροπρέπεια		
* χαυνότης (*vanity*)	μεγαλοψυχία	μικροψυχία	τιμὴν καὶ ἀτιμίαν	
φιλότιμος	[ἀνώνυμος]	ἀφιλότιμος		
ὀργιλότης	πραότης	ἀοργησία	ὀργήν	
ἀλαζονεία	ἀλήθεια	εἰρωνεία	τὸ ἀληθές	
βωμολοχία (*buffoonery*)	εὐτραπελία	ἀγροικία	τὸ ἐν παιδιᾷ ⎫ τὸ ἡδύ ⎱ περὶ λόγων καὶ πράξεων κοινωνίαν	
ἄρεσκος or κόλαξ	φιλία	δύσερις καὶ δύσκολος	κατὰ τὸν βίον ⎭	

* These ἕξεις are similar, but are concerned with small matters (περὶ μικρά) and with great matters (περὶ μεγάλα) respectively.
† e.g. a man might be of a phlegmatic nature and so face danger, not because he is θρασύς, but because he is too dull to realize what he is doing.

In this διαγραφή the extremes are more opposed to one another than to the mean; some extremes actually have a sort of resemblance to the mean, e.g, ἀσωτία to ἐλευθεριότης (prodigality to liberality). It is the extremes only that are strictly contraries, and Aristotle definitely says that it is sometimes the excess, and sometimes the defect, which is most opposed to the mean—ἐγγύτερον καὶ ὁμοιότερον τὸ ἕτερον ἄκρον τῷ μέσῳ. In other words the μ έ σ ο ν *is not half-way*. It is most important to notice this, for otherwise we might think that Aristotle, in this doctrine of the ἠθικαὶ ἀρεταί as μεσότητες, makes a merely quantitative distinction between virtue and vice. This is not so, for a μέσον, which is not in the middle between two extremes, cannot be a μέσον which has anything to do with quantity. The μεσότητες are *qualitative* "means." Aristotle says that they are "hard to hit," and this implies a recognition in his doctrine of what we call the "moral struggle;" it is a big task, he says, to be a good man (διὸ καὶ ἔργον ἐστὶ σπουδαῖον εἶναι), a remark which we may compare with his assertion that virtue is concerned with what is difficult (περὶ τὸ χαλεπώτερον). In this connexion we should notice what he says about the will, and voluntary and involuntary actions. An act done in ignorance is involuntary, we say; but it makes a great difference whether we mean ignorance that we were doing some particular thing, i.e. an unconscious act, or ignorance that such a thing was not a thing to do. This latter kind of ignorance, ἡ ἐν τῇ προαιρέσει ἄγνοια, is not a cause of "involuntary" acts, but of vice; it is an evil man who does not know what he should do and what he should abstain from (ἀγνοεῖ μὲν οὖν πᾶς ὁ μοχθηρὸς ἃ δεῖ πράττειν καὶ ὧν ἀφεκτέον, "Ethics," 1110b, 28).[1]

Voluntary and Involuntary Actions.

---

[1] Compare the Socratic doctrine that ἀρετή = ἐπιστήμη.

The first kind of ignorance, that which produces an "unconscious" act, is an ignorance of the things and persons affected by the act, not an ignorance of the nature of the act itself. It is a "particular" ignorance (of circumstances, etc.), ἡ καθ' ἕκαστα ἄγνοια, and not a general ignorance (ἡ καθόλου ἄγνοια) of the principles involved. Hence Aristotle defines a "voluntary act" as that which originates in oneself, having knowledge of the circumstances (οὗ ἡ ἀρχὴ ἐν αὐτῷ εἰδότι τὰ καθ' ἕκαστα). Seeing that moral actions are concerned with μεσότητες, which are the object of our will and choice (προαίρεσις), both virtue and vice depend upon ourselves. The proverb οὐδεὶς ἑκὼν πονηρὸς οὐδ' ἄκων μακάριος is partly false and partly true: it may be objected that a man's character is such as to be bad, therefore he cannot be blamed even for actions of which the ἀρχή is in himself. But a man is responsible for his character, having made it such by his repeated ἐνέργειαι.

It will be noticed that there is no mention of δικαιοσύνη—the moral virtue *par excellence*, one might think—in the above διαγραφή. This is because Justice is with Aristotle, as it was with Plato, not a "particular" moral virtue, but co-extensive with the whole of virtue. It is, in fact, the highest *expression* of virtue—ἡ τελεία ἀρετή—the realized ἕξις of ἀρετή in man's dealings with his fellow-men. It is essentially πρὸς ἕτερον, a χρῆσις τῆς ἀρετῆς. There is, however, a more limited sense of the word δικαιοσύνη, according to which it is a "particular" virtue, and is the opposite of πλεονεξία.[1] This justice is equivalent to what we mean by "assigning to a man his due," in accordance with his worth (κατ' ἀξίαν); and, just as we speak of "doing unto others as we would be done by," so τὸ

---

[1] The word is not used by Aristotle.

ἀντιπεπονθός—in the sense of τὸ ἀντιπεπονθέναι, suffering oneself what one has inflicted on others—is an essential part of justice in its retributive aspect. But it is not so ἁπλῶς, without qualification, without taking into account all the circumstances, the motive both of the wrong-doer and of society in exacting retribution from him. As Prof. Stewart[1] comments: "'Receiving the same in return' is an erroneous account of distributive justice, because in it the dividend which a man receives ἀπὸ τοῦ κοινοῦ is not the same in kind as the contribution which he makes to the common capital: e.g. the musician is not paid in music, but in money according to his skill. It is also an erroneous account of corrective justice, because it makes punishment merely a matter of immediate personal revenge, ignoring the interests of society, which demand the establishment of an impartial court able to take account of the position and circumstances of the parties as members of the State, and to estimate carefully degrees of responsibility." These considerations caused Aristotle to define it, not as τὸ ἀντιπεπονθός alone, but as τὸ ἀντιπεπονθὸς κατ' ἀναλογίαν, i.e. the suffering of something which is not *identical* with what I have inflicted on another, but something which is, in me, *equivalent* to the injury which I have caused, not only in another individual, but, possibly, in society as a whole.

Aristotle arrives at his account of εὐδαιμονία as the "good" of man by examining the doctrine of Eudoxus, who maintained that pleasure (ἡδονή) is the Good, in that it is οὗ πάντ' ἐφίεται, and if added to any other good (προστιθεμένη) it makes it more desirable. But Plato used exactly this argument to prove that ἡδονή is *not* the Good, and we have already admitted that it must be μὴ συναριθμουμένη, something which

ἡδονή not εὐδαιμονία.

[1] "Notes on Nicomachean Ethics," Vol. I. p. 446.

cannot be equated with other "goods." Moreover, there are different kinds of pleasure; they are qualitatively different (διαφέρουσαι τῷ εἴδει), some better than others, which implies a criterion beyond that of pleasure itself. This standard is supplied by the character of the good man, the σπουδαῖος. The fact that man is not mere sensibility, that his life is πρακτική τις τοῦ λόγον ἔχοντος and not the mere αἰσθητικὴ ζωή, is a sufficient refutation of Hedonism. There are pleasures of the soul—ψυχικαὶ ἡδοναί—as well as pleasures of the body, σωματικαὶ ἡδοναί, which are very different in kind; if they are both "pleasures" they cannot differ in "pleasurableness," but must do so in virtue of some other quality. The best of them resides in the unimpeded activity of man's highest faculties; this, and this alone, constitutes εὐδαιμονία or Happiness. It belongs to the θεωρητικὸς βίος, to the life of contemplation, which is the end and aim of all our activities—that cultivated leisure in which a man finds expression of his finest self, the goal of all his efforts; ἀσχολούμεθα γὰρ ἵνα σχολάζωμεν. This ideal of human life is described by Aristotle as the effort to become as immortal as possible, ἐφ' ὅσον ἐνδέχεται ἀθανατίζειν. By this he means something different from the Christian idea of immortality, which, whatever its nature, is certainly concerned with our life beyond the grave. Aristotle's "immortality" is here and now; it is that realization of ourselves as, in some sense, divine, those moments of "transcendental feeling" to which Plato appeals in his Myths, that uplift of the soul which we feel when brought face to face with the very Presence of Beauty which Diotima describes in the "Symposium" of Plato; it is, as we find in the paraphrase of Eudoxus, the contemplation and service of God—τὸν θεὸν θεραπεύειν καὶ θεωρεῖν. We conclude this section on Aristotle's "Ethics" with his description of this "life":—

But if Happiness is an activity in accordance with virtue, it is reasonable that it should be in accordance with the highest, and this must be that of the best part. Whether this part be the intellect or any other part, which is admitted to rule and lead the other parts naturally, and to contemplate noble and divine things—being either itself divine or the most divine of our faculties—its activity in accordance with its peculiar virtue will be perfect Happiness. We have already said that this activity is speculation. And this would seem to be in conformity both with our former conclusions and with the truth. For this activity is the highest of all (for intellect is the highest of our faculties, and the highest class of knowable things is that with which intellect is concerned); moreover it is the most constant. For we are able to contemplate more constantly than we are able to do any *action*. And we consider that pleasure must accompany Happiness, and it is admitted that of all the activities in accordance with virtue the most pleasurable is that in accordance with wisdom; at least philosophy seems to involve pleasures which are wonderful in respect of their purity and constancy, and it is reasonable that the life of those who possess knowledge should be more pleasurable than that of those who are seeking it. And the requisite independence would seem to belong to speculation more than to anything else. The wise man and the just, and the rest of mankind, need the necessities of life, but when we have been adequately provided with these, the just man needs both means by which, and people upon whom, he can exercise his justice, and it is the same with the temperate and the brave man and the rest of them, whereas the wise man even in solitude can engage in contemplation, and the wiser he is the more he can do so. Perhaps he may do so better, if he has helpers, but still he is the most independent of all. This contemplation would seem to be the only activity loved for its own sake; for nothing results from it beyond contemplation, whereas in the case of the practical activities we gain something, more or less, in addition to the doing of the action. Happiness is considered to reside in leisure; for we busy ourselves that we may have leisure, and wage war that we may have peace. Now the activity of the practical virtues is concerned with military or political affairs, and actions in these spheres seem void of leisure, military actions entirely so (for no one chooses war for war's sake, nor makes preparations for war; a man would be thought a most bloodthirsty person if he were to make enemies of his friends for the sake of having battles and bloodshed); and the activity of political life is also without leisure and is engaged—in addition to actual administration—in gaining power and honour or, at least, happiness for a man's self and the citizens, which is something different from political science, and we obviously desire it as being different. If then of actions in accordance with virtues, the political and military excel in beauty and greatness, but are themselves void of leisure, aiming at some external end and not desirable for their own sakes, while the activity of the intellect, which is contemplation, seems to excel in intensity and to aim at nothing beyond itself, and to have a pleasure of its own—this helps to increase the activity—together with independence and leisure and, humanly speaking, indefatigability, and all the other ingredients of blessedness which are seen to belong to this activity, it follows that this will be man's perfect happiness, so long as the full span of life is granted. For no part of happiness is imperfect. Such a life may seem more than human; for a man will not live this life *qua* man, but in virtue of some divinity within him; but in proportion as this divine part excels man's concrete nature, its activity excels the activities of the other virtues. If then intellect is a divine thing in comparison with a man, the intellectual life is also divine in comparison with human life. We ought not, as some advise, to entertain human thoughts because we are human, or mortal thoughts because we are mortal, but so far as may be to put off our mortality and make every effort to live in accordance with the best that is within us. Though it be small in bulk, it far excels all our other faculties in power and value. And it is this part which would seem to be our real selves, for it is the ruling and better part. It would be absurd for a man to choose the life of some other thing, and not the life of that which is himself. What was said before will hold good here too; for that which is peculiarly suited to each by nature is the highest and most pleasurable thing for each; consequently for man the intellectual life is the most pleasureable, if intellect be the chief mark of man. And so this life is also the happiest (1177a, 12—1178a, 8).

The πόλις.

II. *The Politics of Aristotle.*—All students of Greek history know that the "city-state" (πόλις) is a peculiarly Greek institution; historically considered it is a union of "village communities," a συνοικισμός of κῶμαι, which are collections of families. This is how it comes into being,[1] its ἀρχὴ τῆς κινήσεως. For the sake of protection against wild animals [2]

[1] Theseus, for example, is said to have made the συνοικισμός of Athens.
[2] Cf. the myth from the "Protagoras," above, p. 102.

and, possibly, the attacks of his fellows, primitive man banded himself together in these κῶμαι; then, as civilization advanced, the needs of commerce and the convenience of social intercourse led to the further "banding together" of the πόλις. But this utilitarian origin does not explain its real significance; for that we must look at its τὸ τί ἦν εἶναι. What is it *essentially*? It "comes into being" as we have described; but it exists, or "is," as the environment within which man can realize himself as capable of a life higher than that of the brutes—γιγνομένη μὲν τοῦ ζῆν ἕνεκα, οὖσα δὲ τοῦ εὖ ζῆν is how Aristotle describes it. Man is endowed with a "political" nature, which can only be realized in the πόλις; he is a πολιτικὸν ζῷον. The "final cause" (τὸ οὗ ἕνεκα) of the πόλις is the realization of man's essential nature, and in our examination of a thing we must never neglect this "cause"—ὁρίζεται γάρ ἕκαστον τῷ τέλει. Although, then, historically considered, the individual exists prior to the institution of the πόλις, the πόλις is, logically considered, prior to the individual, as that which is assumed by, or involved in, his existence (πρότερον τῇ φύσει [1] πόλις ἢ οἰκία καὶ ἕκαστος ἡμῶν). This is how Aristotle describes it:

> Since we see that every State is a community, and that every community is established for some good (for all men do everything that they do for the sake of what seems to them to be good), it is clear that all communities aim at some good, and that the community which is the highest of all and includes the rest does so in particular, and aims at the highest good of all. And this is what we call a State or political community.

As to its size, we are told that it must be neither too large nor too small, neither 100,000 men nor 10, but such as can

---

[1] This word has various meanings in Aristotle; here it means "in the essential *nature* of a thing" as considered under the aspect of τὸ τί ἦν εἶναι.

readily be taken in at a glance (εὐσύνοπτος) by which Aristotle really means that it must not be too vast for a man to "find himself" readily within; it must not overwhelm him, but simply provide the environment that gives adequate scope to his personality. In accordance with his usual plan, of considering first the opinions of others, Aristotle is led, before recounting his own ideas, to an examination of the "Republic" of Plato, and makes some adverse criticisms upon the community of wives, of children, and of property, which is there advocated. Plato advocated the community of wives and children for the sake of the unity of the State; but excessive, literal unity is inconsistent with the nature of a πόλις, which is a κοινωνία of a plurality of different elements, kept together by the bond of "reciprocal" equality, i.e. by an equality which takes account of the different services of different individuals to the State. Excessive unity (τὸ λίαν ἐνοῦν τὴν πόλιν) does not recognize these variations, and is, therefore, bad. Moreover, the abolition of the family will result in there being less φιλία in the State, and this is necessary for the inculcating of obedience and the avoidance of revolution. The community of property may sound an ideal thing; κοινὰ τὰ φίλων, as the proverb says, but there are many practical difficulties involved. Without private property one cannot show favour to friends, or give help to strangers, and its existence encourages self-control (σωφροσύνη) in abstaining from what is another's and generosity (ἐλευθεριότης) in dealing with one's own goods. It would therefore seem best to have personal property but a common use of it, whatever this may mean.

Plato's "Republic" criticized.

An examination of the different constitutions which have actually been established in such places as Crete, Sparta, and Athens, leads to the elucidation of three different types

Three Types of Constitutions.

—kingship, aristocracy, and timocracy.[1] Kingship is like the rule of father over son in the family; aristocracy resembles the relations of man to wife; timocracy, those between brothers, who are equal in all except in age. These are "true" forms of government; but there is a perversion corresponding to each. Every true form of government aims at the common good—τὸ κοινῇ συμφέρον—but all the "perversions" are based upon private interest. They are tyranny, oligarchy, and democracy respectively. Both tyranny and kingship are monarchies; the difference between them is that the King is the shepherd of his people, and rules for their sake, whereas the tyrant considers nothing but his own interest. [ὁ μὲν τύραννος τὸ αὐτῷ συμφέρον σκόπει, ὁ δὲ βασιλεὺς τὸ τῶν ἀρχομένων.] The correspondence may be set forth in a table :—

ὀρθὴ πολιτεία	παρέκβασις
1. βασιλεία	τυραννίς
2. ἀριστοκρατία	ὀλιγαρχία (*as when the husband "lords it" over the wife*)
3. πολιτεία [τιμοκρατία]	δημοκρατία (*like a household without a master*)

It will be noticed that δημοκρατία has a different connotation in Aristotle, as with Plato, from what we now regard as the *ideal* of "democracy," however short our realization of it may fall. Our modern use of the word seems to come nearer to the meaning of timocracy in Aristotle, that ὀρθὴ

[1] This last is so-called because it is based upon the principle of allotting power in the State in accordance with a person's worth or τιμή without any consideration of the "accidents" of wealth or birth. Aristotle regards it as, in many ways, the ideal constitution and so terms it simply πολιτεία—the constitution *par excellence*.

πολιτεία which is called πολιτεία simply, than to the meaning of the παρέκβασις, δημοκρατία.[1]

Its characteristics are given as, firstly, the election by lot to all offices in the State from among the whole body of the people without any consideration of a man's qualifications for an office, and, secondly, the payment of members for their services. Freedom (ἐλευθερία) is supposed to be its basis (ὑπόθεσις); but it is a base kind of freedom, the freedom to do as one likes (τὸ ζῆν ὡς βούλεταί τις), which, among modern writers, Matthew Arnold in his "Culture and Anarchy" has exposed as no true freedom at all. True freedom takes into account differences of worth[2]; it is not merely numerical, or "quantitative," but "qualitative"; whereas the ἐλευθερία which is the ὑπόθεσις of δημοκρατία is κατ' ἀριθμὸν ἀλλὰ μὴ κατ' ἀξίαν. It comprises no right conception of equality; because the δῆμος is "equal" in one respect (the freedom to live), it claims equality in all respects, just as oligarchs, because "unequal" in one respect (wealth), claim inequality, i.e. superiority, in all.

In determining what is the best State for ordinary citizens —not, perhaps, the ideal State, but the best that is practically possible—we must be guided by our conception of what is the best life. In the "Ethics" we saw that this consists of ἐνέργειαι κατ' ἀρετήν, and that ἀρετή is a μεσότης; if this is

[1] Compare Plato, above, p. 96.
[2] Compare the Aristotelian idea of distributive Justice as "proportional equality," not simple equality, for the better man is worthy of the better hire. "What is distributively just" may be expressed by a fourfold ratio, or ἀναλογία, in which two terms represent things (or rewards) and two others the persons who are entitled to those things, α : β :: γ : δ. The reward or the remuneration γ is to the reward or remuneration δ as the person α is to the person β, and he who contributes more to the welfare of the State is justly entitled to a greater share in the benefits of the State.

TELEOLOGICAL CONCEPTION OF UNIVERSE

true of the individual, it must apply also to States; for the State or "constitution" (πολιτεία) is only an embodiment of the life of the πόλις—ἡ γὰρ πολιτεία βίος τίς ἐστι πόλεως—an expression of the principles upon which it is organized, just as the πόλις itself is an embodiment of the lives of the individuals within it, the environment within which alone they can "realize" themselves. Our "ethical" conclusions, then, will apply to our "politics." Now of the three classes of "goods,"

1. τὰ ἐκτὸς ἀγαθά (*external goods, such as wealth*)
2. τὰ ἐν τῷ σώματι (*bodily goods, such as health*)
3. τὰ ἐν τῇ ψυχῇ (*moral, intellectual, and spiritual goods*)

we have seen that external goods are only "useful" (χρήσιμα), mere means to an end. It is only the goods of the soul that are ends in themselves, and the "goods" of the three classes stand in the same relation to themselves—are in the same scale of value—as do the things of which they are the "goods." For example, class (3) is as superior to class (2) as the soul is superior to the body; and the best life is the βίος μετ' ἀρετῆς, with just that provision (χορηγία) of external goods which is necessary for its proper realization in external πράξεις. The "ideal State," then, is that in which εὐδαιμονία can find expression. Not all the prerequisite elements of the State will necessarily have a share in the polity—some things are merely ἀναγκαῖα ἐξ ὑποθέσεως, "necessary" in the sense that we cannot do without them, but not entering essentially into the τὸ τί ἦν εἶναι of a thing.[1] Such things are no more parts of a State than a chisel is of a statue, or than any other means is a part of the final cause (τὸ οὗ ἕνεκα). We must, for example, have slaves to perform the menial work, for we

---

[1] Thus some proportion of τὰ ἐκτὸς ἀγαθά, for example, is ἀναγκαῖον ἐξ ὑποθέσεως in the life of the εὐδαίμων.

cannot have our citizens spending their lives in such things (οὐ γὰρ δεῖ βάναυσον βίον ζῆν τοὺς πολίτας).

Education. In the final portion of his "Politics" Aristotle insists upon the importance of education. Εὐδαιμονία, although, perhaps, not entirely independent of τὰ ἐκτὸς ἀγαθά, is not determined by them; as with man, so with States, it is ἐπιστήμη and προαίρεσις which make them good or bad. A man becomes, or is, a good man (σπουδαῖος) owing to three things—φύσις (his natural endowment), ἔθος (habituation, or training), and λόγος (reasoning). Of these three elements φύσις is a factor in determining the character of beasts, ἔθος also, with some animals; but λόγος is the peculiarly human factor. Of the two parts of the human soul, the rational and intellectual (τὸ λόγον ἔχον καθ' αὑτό) and the volitional (τὸ λόγῳ ὑπάκουον), the first determines the τέλος for the second, for the inferior always exists for the sake of the superior, war for the sake of peace, ἀσχολία for the sake of σχόλη, and, indeed, all ἀναγκαῖα καὶ χρήσιμα for the sake of τὰ καλά. The law-giver must consider all these things, but especially τὰ καλά, and education must look to this. The Spartan is an example of the neglect of this principle; being trained only for war, he fails when not at war, οὐ δυνάμενος σχολάζειν. Education must therefore be a State affair, for it is too important to entrust to private enterprise. Aristotle lays down a fourfold curriculum:—

1. ἡ γραμματική
2. ἡ γραφική
3. ἡ μουσική
4. ἡ γυμναστική

of which the last is directed towards the production of bravery (ἀνδρεία)—the essentially manly quality—and must not, therefore, have its efforts baulked by any effeminacy

TELEOLOGICAL CONCEPTION OF UNIVERSE 135

caused by (3), which must not, therefore, be pursued ἡδονῆς χάριν. Of (1) and (2) the art of writing has a merely utilitarian object; idealism is provided for in the second (and also the third). Μουσική and γυμναστική were the two traditional sides of Greek education, and μουσική is, of course, far wider than "music." It is, in fact, "the humanities," as we call them, an essential part of that cultivated leisure which is the Greek ideal. In time, γυμναστική must come first; the body must be trained before the mind, but not—as at Sparta—at the expense of the mind. This is followed by μουσική, which is both a moral discipline and an intellectual enjoyment. Aristotle gives great emphasis to it as a moral discipline; it makes for virtue, he says, (τείνει πρὸς ἀρετήν), because, just as γυμναστική gives a certain tone to the body, so μουσική gives a tone to the temperament (ποῖόν τι ποιεῖ τὸ ἦθος). In other words, it trains the taste, teaches men to take pleasure in what is beautiful and to be pained by what is ugly—whether morally or æsthetically—which recalls the quotation from Plato in the "Ethics"[1] that a man must be trained to find pleasure and sorrow in the objects in which he should (ὥστε χαίρειν τε καὶ λυπεῖσθαι οἷς δεῖ).

(III) *The Psychology of Aristotle.*—We have seen how the doctrines laid down by Aristotle in his "Ethics" inform his "Politics" as well—just as we saw the psychology of Plato repeated in *his* politics—and, although Aristotle wrote a special treatise on psychology,[2] we must not expect a rigid division between this and other aspects of his teaching; his psychology is, in fact, very intimately bound up with his metaphysics.

Psychology, as the name implies, is the science of the soul.

---
[1] 1104b, 12.
[2] The περὶ ψυχῆς or De Anima, as it is commonly called by its Latin title.

Long ago the Sophists taught us—by implication and criticism rather than by explicit teaching—that in our search for knowledge we must not take φαινόμενα for granted; they are, in some sense, relative to a percipient subject; there is a subjective as well as an objective factor in all knowledge. We must therefore not only direct our gaze towards the external universe, but also turn our eyes inward upon ourselves. We must be mindful of *What is man?* Just as all objects are combinations of matter (ὕλη) and form (μορφή), so man himself is a compound nature (σύνθετος οὐσία), a union of matter and form, of body and soul, and of these two it is the soul that gives to man his real significance. We are already familiar with the Aristotelian doctrine that the inferior exists for the sake of the superior; if then the soul is superior to the body, the latter may be said to exist for the sake of the former. In other words, the soul is the "final cause" of the body; and it is also its "efficient cause," for the body is set in motion by it.[1] Moreover, it is also the "formal cause"—τὸ τί ἦν εἶναι [2]—of the body, that which, as we have just said, gives to man his real significance. The soul is spiritual, in the sense that the body is material; a living body is very different from the most life-like statue; a statue may have the external form of the human body, but it has not that which gives real significance to the body, that which it essentially *is*; it has not got soul, which is the τὸ τί ἦν εἶναι of the body, as Aristotle says in his "Metaphysics," or the "actuality" of the body (ἐντελέχεια τοῦ σώματος), as he puts it in the present treatise.

The Soul.

Now can we give any scientific account of this "soul"?

[1] "Motion" is not only spatial change, but includes quantitative growth and also qualitative development.
[2] "Metaphysics," 1035b, 16.

It may be regarded under three aspects, or as having three "parts."[1]

1. τὸ θρεπτικόν — Common to plants, animals, and men.
2. τὸ αἰσθητικόν — Common to man and all animals. It is sometimes called τὸ ὀρεκτικόν, because "perception" produces "desire;" "desire" is impossible without αἴσθησις. Sometimes also the phrase κινητικὸν κατὰ τόπον is used to describe that which is common to man and most animals.
3. τὸ διανοητικόν — Peculiar to man.

The identity of this table with the corresponding ζωαί which we saw at the beginning of the "Ethics" will not escape notice.

We need say nothing about the "nutritive" part of the soul; but τὸ αἰσθητικόν calls for a few remarks, for it involves an examination of "sense-perception" in a way more akin to our modern associations of the word *psychology* than does anything else in the account so far given of the soul. The nature of αἴσθησις, says Aristotle, is not properly understood in the popular view, which regards it as a form of transformation (ἀλλοίωσις) involving passive impression (τὸ πάσχειν)[2]. But we must distinguish two senses of πάσχειν: it may involve the destruction of a thing by something which is the opposite of it, as when pleasure banishes sorrow from the mind, or health disease from the body; or it may involve the modification only of a thing, and such modification may amount

αἴσθησις.

[1] Aristotle understood Plato to make an *actual*, and not merely *logical*, division of the soul into three parts, but himself guards against such a misapprehension in the words λόγῳ μόνον χωριστόν.

[2] The reader will recall the early Empedoclean theory of ἀπόρροιαι which impinge upon the eye and make us perceive "like by like" (see above, p. 38).

to the bringing to full development of something which was latent in the one body until aroused into actuality by the action of the other, something which previously existed potentially (δυνάμει), but not actually (ἐνεργείᾳ or ἐντελεχείᾳ). This is the distinction which Aristotle makes between

(a) φθορά τις ὑπὸ τοῦ ἐναντίου, and

(b) σωτηρία τις τοῦ δυνάμει ὄντος ὑπὸ τοῦ ἐντελεχείᾳ ὄντος,

and (b) cannot rightly be called an ἀλλοίωσις. This is the element in sense-perception which is contributed by the percipient subject,[1] and makes αἴσθησις not a mere act of passive receptivity. Here at last we can strike a true balance between the claims of the "subjective" and the "objective" factor in the building up of our knowledge. Perception is not the mere passivity of the sense-organ, but the functioning of αἴσθησις *through* the sense-organ. Its object is implicitly a universal, a τοιόνδε τι and not a mere τόδε τι. The senses may be our only means of perception, but it would be more correct to say that we perceive *through* them, rather than by them. They are the channels which lead to the πρῶτον αἰσθητήριον of the soul, where the "perception" really takes place.[2] This is illustrated by the fact that, although the particular senses, such as sight and hearing, have their own individual objects (ἴδια αἰσθητά)—such as colours and sounds—there are also "common sensibles" (κοινὰ αἰσθητά) which can be perceived by more than one faculty, e.g. movement, which can be perceived by both sight and touch.

νοῦς. Aristotle's treatment of "thought" in the "De Anima" gives scope for a variety of interpretations, but it will be sufficient to put the matter very simply here. We may ex-

[1] In some sense, then, the external object is not the *cause*, but the *occasion*, of the perception.

[2] Cf. the doctrine in the "Theætetus" of Plato, above p. 111.

press the difference between sensation and thought by an ἀναλογία of the following kind :—

sensation : thought : : concrete : abstract.

Sensation enables us to know the immediate phenomenon (e.g. σάρξ); by thought we realize its essential nature, τὸ σαρκὶ εἶναι.[1] And just as in sensation there is a purely passive and a more active element, so it is with thought (νοῦς). It has both a "passive" and an "active" function, and is called νοῦς παθητικός in virtue of its ability to acquire all kinds of knowledge, to be affected, that is, by all kinds of perceptions (τῷ πάντα γίνεσθαι); but it has also an active function in virtue of its ability to interpret, as it were, to "make" all kinds of perceptions (τῷ πάντα ποιεῖν). This ability of the mind is, indeed, one of the pre-suppositions of αἴσθησις itself. It is true that we cannot think without having something to think about; thought requires an object suggested by sense— νοεῖν οὐκ ἔστιν ἄνευ φαντάσματος—but it is equally true that thought requires to illumine this object in order to think it.[2]

(IV) *Aristotle's Logic and Theory of Knowledge.*—It will be remembered that Pre-Socratic philosophy was much exercised about what we may call predication troubles :[3] does the *copula* "is" denote existence? does it assert identity between the two terms related by it? The Pre-Socratics regarded existence (τὰ ὄντα) as identical with the sensible world, and those who carried the doctrine of *flux*—οἱ φάσκοντες ἡρακλειτίζειν, as Aristotle remarks [4]—to its logical extreme, as Cratylus did, held that we ought not to say anything, but

---

[1] The phrase is equivalent to an abstract noun, just as ἀγαθόν is *good* and τὸ ἀγαθῷ εἶναι is "the being good" or *goodness*.

[2] Thus again is the balance struck between the "subjective" and the "objective."

[3] See above, p. 48.   [4] "Metaphysics," 1010a, 11.

content ourselves with moving a finger. Parmenides and Zeno reduced things to such a logical *impasse* that the meaning of " is " had to be cleared up before any advance was possible. This was, of course, done by Plato, whose later " intellectual " dialogues are a great contribution to the theory of knowledge; but Aristotle is the first—consistently with his more precise and orderly type of mind—to put the matter in a " cut and dried " form, and so we have reserved it for explicit mention here.

There are several senses in which we may say that one thing *is* something else, and these are set forth by Aristotle in his "forms of predication," or "categories," as they are generally styled—τὰ σχήματα τῆς κατηγορίας.[1] There are ten of these categories, i.e. ten possible meanings of the word " is " in the statement *a is b*. If it defines the nature, or substance, of *a* (i.e. tells us what it *is*), it falls under the first category of substance (τί ἐστι); but it may only define a quality of *a*, when it falls under the category of quality (ποιόν); or it may tell us how large or small it is, when it comes under that of quantity (ποσόν), and so on. The next most important category is that of relation (πρός τι), as when we say that Critias is a disciple of Socrates. The other six are those of place, time, activity, passivity, state (κεῖσθαι), e.g. a man is sitting down, and condition (ἔχειν), e.g. a man has his armour on.[2] Thus is the ambiguity of that troublesome little word *is* once and for all cleared up.

τὰ σχήματα τῆς κατηγορίας.

συλλογισμός.

Aristotle is the first writer to attempt a scientific account of thought-processes. In his " Prior Analytics " he deals with the " syllogism," which is thus defined : συλλογισμὸς δέ ἐστι λόγος ἐν ᾧ τεθέντων τινῶν ἕτερόν τι τῶν κειμένων ἐξ ἀνάγκης

---
[1] " Metaphysics," 1017a, 23, and " Categories " [iv.], 6.
[2] These last two do not seem to differ very much.

TELEOLOGICAL CONCEPTION OF UNIVERSE 141

συμβαίνει τῷ ταῦτα εἶναι—a syllogism is a method of reasoning in which from certain presuppositions something else different from the premises necessarily follows from their truth.[1] The syllogism is of the familiar form—

All men are mortal,
Socrates is a man,
∴ Socrates is mortal,

and is not of much use in the acquisition of knowledge, though it is the common form of the proof (ἀπόδειξις) of anything. In our search for knowledge induction (ἐπαγωγή) is ἐπαγωγή. of far greater importance than deduction, and we have already found Socrates normally employing it.[2] It is an argument from the particular to the general, concluding from the fact that something is true in this and that case, in all cases known to us, that it is therefore universally true. Such an "induction by simple enumeration," as it is called, can never be exhaustive, and is open, as Bacon pointed out, to refutation by a single "contrary instance." But it is a mistake to imagine that Aristotle thought we could argue thus from particulars to universals. Let us examine one of those ἐπακτικοὶ λόγοι of which he approved so much in the διαλεκτική of Socrates. There is a very simple one in the early chapters of the "Republic."[3] Thrasymachus has been maintaining that it is just to help one's friends and harm one's enemies. Socrates thinks that the just man will not do harm to anyone, and proceeds thus: Horses which suffer harm become worse *qua* horses; dogs which suffer harm become worse *qua* dogs; men who suffer harm become worse *qua* men; justice is the human ἀρετή *par excellence*, and so men who suffer harm become more unjust, i.e. justice makes

---

[1] "Analytics," 24b, 18.   [2] See above, p. 60.   [3] 335b.

men more unjust, which is absurd. Here the proof does not really rest upon the three particular instances of horses, dogs, and men, but rather upon the universal principle, *implicitly admitted*, that harm is a bad thing and anything harmed becomes *ipso facto* worse. And so it is generally with Aristotle's use of ἐπαγωγή, which therefore does not lie open to Bacon's criticism.

We find the same thing at the bottom of Aristotle's theory of knowledge, which, in spite of what, at first glance, seems its more empirical nature, does not really differ very much from Plato's. We have seen already[1] three elements of Plato's epistemology—the distinction between ὀρθὴ δόξα and ἐπιστήμη, the doctrine of ἀνάμνησις, and the Ideas—and it is unnecessary to repeat them here. Now Aristotle's greatest contention is that scientific knowledge is demonstrated truth; induction may collect facts, but it is deduction which ἀπόδειξις. is the real proof (ἀπόδειξις). We know a thing scientifically when we know the reason for it, the διότι and not the mere ὅτι. But all truths cannot be thus demonstrated to be true because of the truth of something else; this would lead to an "infinite regress," or to an all-inclusive circular proof. We must eventually come to some ultimate principles, the truth of which we perceive, so to speak, intuitively, and these indemonstrable first principles (ἀναπόδεικτοι ἀρχαί)—e.g. that the nature of number is such that $2 + 2 = 4$—are the foundation of his ἀπόδειξις, just as his ἐπαγωγή really rests upon the admission of the truth of a principle which the instances merely illustrate but do not prove.

(V) *The Metaphysics of Aristotle.*—We have already dealt with a variety of themes that come within the scope of this treatise, for it deals with the most general or universal aspect

[1] Above, pp. 104-111.

TELEOLOGICAL CONCEPTION OF UNIVERSE 143

of philosophy—ἡ πρώτη φιλοσοφία—in the sense given to it at the beginning of this book, with that reflection or speculation to which we are led by our inability to find an explanation of the universe within the physical sphere; our "physical" speculations lead beyond themselves, as it were, to something else, to metaphysics (τὰ μετὰ τὰ φυσικά). It is the science that studies those πρῶται ἀρχαί or four "causes" which have already proved so useful to us.[1] It will be unnecessary now to say much more about three of these four; but we must examine a little more closely what is the nature of the "formal cause" (τὸ τί ἦν εἶναι), which seems to be equivalent to what Plato designated by his ἰδέα. It is remarkable to note that in the fourth book of his "Metaphysics,"[2] which is an elaborate list of definitions of philosophical terms, Aristotle himself uses the words εἶδος and οὐσία —form and essence—in reference to it, and recognises, in his survey of previous philosophical speculations, in the first book, that the Platonists came nearest, among all his predecessors, to the conception which he designated by it: τὸ δὲ τί ἦν εἶναι καὶ τὴν οὐσίαν σαφῶς μὲν οὐδεὶς ἀποδέδωκε, μάλιστα δ' οἱ τὰ εἴδη τιθέντες.[3] Nay, he actually defines it by the words εἶδος and παράδειγμα in the official definition of the fourth book: τὸ εἶδος καὶ τὸ παράδειγμα, τοῦτο δ' ἐστὶν ὁ λόγος τοῦ τί ἦν εἶναι.[4] We reach the same conclusion if we examine what Aristotle called his "universals;" these are not particular substances, which have existence by themselves, but predicative concepts applicable to many individual objects (τὸ καθόλου καθ' ὑποκειμένου τινὸς λέγεται ἀεί)[5]—the universal is always predicable of some subject. There cannot be particular "existence" of a universal—οὐδὲν τῶν καθόλου ὑπαρχόντων

τὸ τί ἦν εἶναι

[1] See above, p. 6. [2] 1015a, 10.
[3] "Metaphysics," 988a, 35. [4] 1013a, 27. [5] 1038b, 16.

οὐσία ἐστί[1]—and no universal, or "common predicate," designates a particular as such, a τόδε τι, but a particular in virtue, as Plato would say, of its "participation" in the idea, or, as Aristotle says, in virtue of its being also a τοιόνδε τι (οὐδὲν σημαίνει τῶν κοινῇ κατηγορουμένων τόδε τι, ἀλλὰ τοιόνδε[2] —no common predicate indicates a "this," but rather a "such"). Just as Plato regarded his ideas as eternal, not affected, that is to say, by the "coming into being" or destruction of any particular phenomena, but independent (χωριστά) of such vicissitudes, so Aristotle regards his universal—so essential to the possibility of definition at all—as independent of φθορά and γένεσις: a particular house may be built or demolished, but my "concept" of house does not come into being or vanish therewith (οὐ γὰρ γίγνεται τὸ οἰκίᾳ εἶναι ἀλλὰ τὸ τῇδε τῇ οἰκίᾳ[3]). Without such ideas—Platonic ideas, as it seems to me—there can be no knowledge in the sense of ἐπιστήμη (ἄνευ μὲν γὰρ τοῦ καθόλου οὐκ ἔστιν ἐπιστήμην λαβεῖν,)[4] but only vague impressions of sense to which the Heraclitean doctrine of flux would entitle us. So far as the "theory of predication" is concerned, Aristotle's "universals" and Plato's "ideas" serve the same purpose. When we say "Man is an animal" we mean, in modern logic, that our concept of "man" includes that of "animal"—the concept "man" is a particular instance of the concept "animal" —Plato would say that man μετέχει, or participates in, the idea of animal. Aristotle says that man is one of the class "animals," and the only difference—apart from the verbal one—between him and Plato is a difference in the assumptions, or presuppositions, of his whole philosophical system rather than in his analysis of the proposition. For Aristotle regarded the world as composed of a fixed number of "natural

[1] 1038b, 35. [2] 1039a, 1. [3] 1039b, 25. [4] 1086b, 5.

kinds"—concrete and definite divisions in Nature, which it is the object of our knowledge to discover and to classify properly, i.e. as they actually *are* grouped in the external world. Thus Aristotle takes a somewhat more objective view of things than Plato does[1]—just as Sophists like Protagoras took a more subjective view than Plato did. Plato's exposition seems nearer to the truth than either, at any rate so far as the building-up of our knowledge is concerned—which has more to do with the right framing of our "concepts" than with the discovery of "natural kinds."

But let us turn to broader issues. We saw, when considering Aristotle's psychology, how he maintained that the soul was the ἀρχὴ κινήσεως of the body,[2] and this discovery of the source of motion is a most far-reaching one, for we have seen that the great objection to materialism is its inability to explain motion or to account for life. Stretch out your hand and move a finger to and fro; now, when you come to think about it, is not that a very wonderful thing? Obviously your body is "material"—you can touch it, and cut it—but it is a very wonderful material, informed and made different from all inanimate material by the soul or spirit. What can we say about this? Aristotle calls it ἀκίνητος οὐσία, which is not itself "moved," but is the cause of motion in the limbs. It must be eternal, or it would have been "brought into being" by something else; then we should have to ask what brought the "something else" into being, and so we should have an infinite regress of causes, positing ἀρχὴ κινήσεως behind ἀρχὴ κινήσεως for ever. And, if thus eternal, it must be immaterial, for all matter is subject to

Motion.

---

[1] It is this general trend of his mind which, most likely, prevented him from seeing the similarity of his τὸ τί ἦν εἶναι to Plato's ἰδέα.
[2] Above, p. 136.

"coming into being" and to decay. We must believe, then, in a "first cause" the essence of which is energy (ἐνέργεια) —δεῖ ἄρα εἶναι ἀρχὴν τοιαύτην ἧς ἡ οὐσία ἐνέργεια.[1] It is essentially—which is to say, by the very essence of the case —" energy," ἐνέργεια—"life." Aristotle describes this—you may call it God, spirit, or what you will—as ὃ οὐ κινούμενον κινεῖ, and explains how it does so from the analogy of human desire (κινεῖ δὲ ὧδε τὸ ὀρεκτὸν καὶ τὸ νοητόν[2]). Desire for a thing causes me to strive after it, or a "notion" or "idea" that I have formed directs, and indeed originates, all my endeavours; but one could not say that the desire or the notion is "moved," though it is the cause of motion in me —κινεῖ οὐ κινούμενον. Similarly with regard to the universal spirit of the world; it is the cause of motion as being that which is aimed at, the "final cause" of all things; it moves by being loved—κινεῖ δὲ ὡς ἐρώμενον."[3]

[Marginal note: "God."]

This is how Aristotle describes it :—

> On such a principle, then, depend the heavens and the world of nature. And its life is such as the best which we enjoy, and enjoy for but a short time. For it is ever in this state (which we cannot be) since its actuality is also pleasure. (And therefore [sc. because they are activities or actualities] are waking, perception, and thinking most pleasant, and hopes and memories are so because of their reference to these.) And thought in itself deals with that which is best in itself, and that which is thought in the fullest sense with that which is best in the fullest sense. And thought thinks itself because it shares the nature of the object of thought; for it becomes an object of thought in coming into contact with and thinking its objects, so that thought and object of thought are the same. For that which is *capable* of receiving the object of thought, i.e. the essence, is thought. And it is *active* when it *possesses* this object. Therefore the latter <possession> rather than the former <receptivity> is the divine element which thought seems to contain, and the act of contemplation is what is most pleasant and best. If, then, God is always in that good state

---

[1] "Metaphysics," 1071b, 20.   [2] 1071b, 26.   [3] 1072b, 3.

in which we sometimes are, this compels our wonder; and if in a better, this compels it yet more. And God *is* in a better state. And life also belongs to God; for the actuality of thought is life, and God is that actuality; and God's essential actuality is life most good and eternal. We say, therefore, that God is a living being, eternal, most good, so that life and duration continuous and eternal belong to God; for this *is* God . . . (1072b, 14-30).

It is clear, then, from what has been said that there is a substance which is eternal and unmovable, and separate from sensible things. It has been shown also that this substance cannot have any magnitude, but is without parts and indivisible. For it produces movement through infinite time, but nothing finite has infinite power. And, while every magnitude is either infinite or finite, it cannot, for the above reason, have finite magnitude, and it cannot have infinite magnitude because there is no infinite magnitude at all. But it is also clear that it is impassive and unalterable, for all other changes are posterior to change of place <i.e. impossible without>. It is clear, then, why the first mover has these attributes . . . (1073a, 3-13).

Our forefathers in the most remote ages have handed down to us their posterity, a tradition, in the form of a myth, that these substances are gods and that the divine encloses the whole of nature. The rest of the tradition has been added later in mythical form with a view to the persuasion of the multitude, and to its legal and utilitarian expediency; they say these gods are in the form of men or like some of the other animals, and they say other things consequent on and similar to these which we have mentioned. But if we were to separate the first point from these additions and take it alone—that they thought the first substances to be gods, we must regard this as an inspired utterance, and reflect that, while probably each art and science has often been developed as far as possible and has again perished, these opinions have been preserved until the present, like relics of the ancient treasure. Only thus far, then, is the opinion of our ancestors and our earliest predecessors clear to us.

The nature of the divine thought involves certain problems; for while thought is held to be the most divine of things observed by us, the question what it must be in order to have that character involves difficulties. For if it thinks nothing, what is there here of dignity? It is just like one who sleeps. And if it thinks, but this depends on something else, then (as that which is its substance is not the act of thinking, but a potency), it cannot be the best substance; for it is through thinking that its value belongs to it. Further, whether its substance is the faculty of thought or the act of thinking, what does it think? Either itself or something else; and if something else, either the same always or something different. Does it matter, then, or not, whether it thinks the good or any chance thing? Are there not some things about which it is incredible that it should think? Evidently, then, it thinks that which is most divine and precious, and it does not change; for change would be change for the worse, and this would be already a movement. First, then, if "thought" is not the act of thinking, but a potency, it would be reasonable to suppose that the continuity of its thinking is wearisome to it. Secondly, there would evidently be something else more precious than thought, viz. that which is thought. For both thinking and the act of thought will belong even to one who has the worst of thoughts. Therefore if this ought to be avoided (and it ought, for there are even some things which it is better not to see than to see), the act of thinking cannot be the best of things. Therefore it must be itself that thought thinks (since it is the most excellent of things), and its thinking is a thinking on thinking.[1] (1074b, 1-35).

There is no difference here between Aristotle and Plato's conception of the soul as ἀρχὴ κινήσεως, and who, if he did not know that it was Aristotle's, would hesitate to attribute the following remark to Plato?—ὅτι μὲν οὖν ἔστιν οὐσία τις ἀΐδιος καὶ ἀκίνητος καὶ κεχωρισμένη τῶν αἰσθητῶν,[2] φανερὸν ἐκ τῶν εἰρημένων.[3] It is in this one principle—οὐσία ἀΐδιος, ὁ οὐ κινούμενον κινεῖ—that we find the Unity of the world of which we first heard among the Eleatics. It belongs not to the material, but to the spiritual, sphere, for unity of principles is a good, just as a diversity is bad. "Οὐκ ἀγαθὸν πολυκοιρανίη, εἷς κοίρανος ἔστω," as Aristotle quotes from Homer.[4]

Whatever we may make of Aristotle's words—and they are, as perhaps the nature of the subject necessarily entails, somewhat vague—there can be no doubt that they involve conceptions inconsistent with the popular idea of the limita-

---
[1] Translated by W. D. Ross (Oxford Translations of Aristotle).
[2] I.e. separate from sensible things.
[3] "Metaphysics," 1073a, 3.   [4] "Iliad," II. 204.

TELEOLOGICAL CONCEPTION OF UNIVERSE 149

tions of pagan philosophy. Aristotle, as has been remarked,[1] "might, indeed, seem to coincide with the utterance of the Psalmist, 'What is man in comparison with the Heavens?' But with him the Heavens were not a mere physical creation; rather the eternal sphere of Reason, the abode of pure Intelligences, the source of all emanations of Reason and Intelligence throughout the world. Compared with this higher sphere individual man, with his practical and moral life, appeared insignificant; and yet the End-in-itself, even for the individual, Aristotle acknowledged to be worth an effort, while man in organized societies, in the city or the nation, he recognized as affording scope for the realization of something more noble and divine.... The individual man, according to Aristotle, shared in that Reason, which is the divinest part of the Universe, and by development of this into philosophy he could become like to God (see 'Ethics,' X. 7, 8).[2] Thus there were two human things about which Aristotle could be enthusiastic—the life of an ideally well-ordered State, and the moments of philosophical consciousness in the mind of an individual thinker." Prof. Stewart comments to the same effect:[3] "The form of God is realized in one Eternal Being: the form of man in a multitude of contemporary and successive examples. Each individual man realizes himself only by looking away from his own mere particularity, and assimilating into his consciousness the form of man's reason as other examples—his friends and fellow-citizens—by their cumulative influence impress it more purely upon him. The great embodiment of human

---

[1] Grant, "Ethics of Aristotle," Vol. I. p. 286.
[2] The reference is to the ἐφ' ὅσον ἐνδέχεται ἀθανατίζειν quoted above (see p. 126).
[3] "Notes on the Nicomachean Ethics," Vol. II. p. 387.

reason, the social order into which he has been born, exists independently of himself. It is there already as an object for him to contemplate and identify himself with. . . . To contemplate, and in contemplating to identify himself with, the social life is a thing which a man can do almost continuously, because his οὐσία or φύσις is to be a person who sees himself in others and lives in others. But to identify himself with νοητά which involve no social reference is a godlike act, which he can only at rare intervals, and for a short time, perform." We give yet another quotation from the same illuminating commentator. " In man's composite nature the principle of Form asserts itself with difficulty against Matter. Νόησις, the purest expression of this principle, cannot be long kept up, for it is soon checked, and the pleasure attending it destroyed, by the resistance of the material part of his nature. Before νόησις can be resumed, and its attendant pleasure experienced again, the material resistance must have had time to subside—matter must have its own way, for a while, and be allowed its own pleasure. Thus the life of the individual man is broken up into short periods of νόησις, properly so-called, alternating with times during which the material vehicle asserts itself on its own account; and this experience of the individual is paralleled, on a great scale, in the life of the race, the specific form of which is not realized in one immortal individual, but asserts itself, more or less perfectly, for a short time in the adults of one generation, is eclipsed by their decay and death, regains force in their young descendants, and again asserts itself, more or less perfectly, in these when they reach adult age. But God is not thus discrete, like the higher moments of man, or the individuals of a species." [1]

[1] Stewart, "Notes on the Nicomachean Ethics," Vol. II. p. 259.

TELEOLOGICAL CONCEPTION OF UNIVERSE

We remarked just now that these conceptions seem inconsistent with the popular idea of the limitations of pagan philosophy; they will not, however, surprise the reader for whom this book is intended, and we will conclude by reminding him of his reading in Virgil:—

> Principio cælum ac terram camposque liquentes
> lucentemque globum lunæ Titaniaque astra
> spiritus intus alit, totamque infusa per artus
> mens agitat molem et magno se corpore miscet.
> inde hominum pecudumque genus vitæque volantum
> et quæ marmoreo fert monstra sub æquore pontus.
> igneus est ollis vigor et cælestis origo
> seminibus, quantum non corpora noxia tardant
> terreniqui hebetant artus moribundaque membra.
> hinc metuunt cupiuntque, dolent gaudentque, neque auras
> dispiciunt clausæ tenebris et carcere cæco.
>
> ("Æneid," VI. 724-734.)

Manilius,[1] who, though not generally read in schools, has ideas so similar that a few lines must be quoted here, says:—

> namque canam tacita naturam mente potentem
> infusumque deum cælo terrisque fretoque
> ingentem æquali moderantem fœdere molem,
> totumque alterno consensu vivere mundum
> et rationis agi motu, cum spiritus unus
> per cunctas habitet partis atque irriget orbem
> omnia pervolitans corpusque animale figuret.
>
> (II. 61-67.)

and again, more explicitly,

> at manet incolumis mundus suaque omnia servat,
> quæ nec longa dies auget minuitque senectus,
> nec motus puncto curvat, cursusque fatigat;
> idem semper erit, quoniam semper fuit idem.
> non alium videre patres, aliumve nepotes
> aspicient: deus est, qui non mutatur in ævum.
>
> (I. 525-530.)

---

[1] Poet and astronomer who "flourished" about A.D. 8.

CONCLUSION

IN the concluding portion of the last chapter we insensibly passed from the sphere of knowledge to that of religion; and, although this is not—in the accepted sense—a religious work, it will not be out of place to try to determine the extent to which knowledge can—and, for some of us, must—enter into our religion.[1] Religion, it is true, transcends knowledge; and even in the sphere which is common to both, religion carries a certain warmth and fervour with it, which contrasts strongly with the cold light of the intellect. It is the passionate apprehension of things, not only by the intellect, but also by the imagination; and yet, in so far as it is apprehension, that "apprehension" must be made in the same way as we "apprehend" anything else. Consequently we must examine that part of religion which consists of knowledge by the ordinary *criteria* of truth, without any reference to "revelation." What is commonly called "revealed truth" is so different in nature from what we associate with the Aristotelian ἀπόδειξις that the epithet seems almost to have robbed the substantive of all meaning.

Matthew Arnold defined religion as "morality tinged with emotion;" but this seems to be only a half-truth; for "morality" to modern ears, at least, does not connote any

[1] On this subject G. Lowes Dickinson's excellent little volume, "Religion: a Criticism and a Forecast," in Dent's "Modern Problems" series, should be read.

intellectual apprehension of things, and we cannot accept a definition which allots no place to man's highest faculties, to the διανοητικὸν μέρος of the soul, to that θεῖόν τι in us, which Aristotle calls νοῦς. That this is so may be seen from a consideration of two incontestable facts, (1) that the religious views of most of us are considerably modified by our education, (2) that we feel when we read Plato that he is one of the world's greatest religious teachers. If "morality" meant all that we have seen to be connoted by the Socratic formula ἀρετή = ἐπιστήμη, then the definition might stand; but, as it is, we must add to it something like *and knowledge passionately imagined*. By this we mean knowledge which becomes a part of us, which no longer remains information, but enters into our very souls and helps to make us something different from what we were before we acquired it. It is something which we commonly *feel* rather than *think*; but, nevertheless, it does admit of ἀπόδειξις, when called for. We may have difficulties in expressing it in words, difficulties which lead us to resort to mythological language—just as Plato will leave intellectual arguments and lapse into a myth—but we must never interpret our mythology literally, any more than we would take a Platonic myth literally. The mythology is not part of the truth, but a device to bring the truth home to our feeling, a sort of πειθοῦς δημιουργός. So it is always with Plato; feeling, as we have said, comes in as a sort of guarantee of the rightness of thought. But the thought must be there, and must, to some extent, admit of ἀπόδειξις.

When we reflect upon some of the developments of religion to-day, we are inclined to imagine that the element of "feeling" has almost ousted "thought" from its true domain; so that we really need a reconstruction of religion which shall strike the balance between feeling and thought, much as Socrates and Plato struck the balance between the subjective and the objective elements, alike in our knowledge and in our ethics, after the Sophists had laid such emphasis upon the subjective side. Feeling is of vast importance; knowledge which leaves us cold is of no use. "The tigers of wrath are wiser than the horses of instruction," says Blake;[1] but the present age is one which rather needs the stress to be put upon the other half of the truth—that feeling, without thought to guide it, easily "runs amuck;" that enthusiasm and the will-for-good may be all we can expect from the crowd, but its leaders must have intelligence—ναρθηκοφόροι μὲν πολλοί, βάκχοι δέ τε παῦροι.[2]

The brief examination in this book of the development of philosophical speculation among the Greeks showed us roughly the following facts. Man's first attitude towards things is a theological one; anything which he cannot understand he puts down to the account of some *god* or *dæmon*. A mythology is gradually evolved, largely through the influence of poets, which, though often very crude and primitive, yet *is the repository of a certain amount of religious feeling*. We must never interpret such a mythology literally, or we shall miss its whole significance from a religious point of view, which is, briefly, simply this— that man finds something superhuman in his environment, something which passeth his understanding; and this feeling the poets and other great minds of the age body forth in legends which, however literally they may be interpreted by the undiscerning mind, are, to the poets and seers who formulated them, figurative expressions of the great mystery of life. The literal interpreta-

[1] In "The Marriage of Heaven and Hell."
[2] Plato, "Phædo," 69c.

tion which was, no doubt, often given to these legends strengthens a latent scepticism among the more reflective minds, and this leads by a swing of the pendulum to a frank materialism. But materialism, as we have seen, cannot explain motion, and so it interests us no longer. Reflection upon ourselves shows us that we are composite natures, unions of body and soul, of the material and the spiritual. With this recognition of a spiritual force in the world theology comes into its own once more, and busies itself with man's highest conceptions of immortality and of God. Let us examine these two conceptions.

That we have a soul we cannot doubt; nor can we doubt that it is immortal in the same sense as the body is mortal. This necessarily amounts to a belief in a certain kind of immortality; but so far as our *knowledge* of that immortality goes it does not involve anything which can rightly be called *personal* immortality. The greatest minds in all ages have been inclined to such a *belief;* Plato, for example, when he wrote the "Phædo" at least, would seem to have believed in it; but the immortality of which he had knowledge, which admits of ἀπόδειξις, is not an immortality of particular souls, but rather an immortality of universal soul—the everlastingness of the spiritual force in the world, which inspires generations of men in their turn, and into which all are absorbed at death. So much Plato, and others after him, has convincingly proved, but we must not forget that such an "immortality of soul" does not necessarily prove the "immortality of souls." That my soul will survive death does not necessarily mean that I shall be conscious of the fact, for I am not my soul, but a σύνθετος οὐσία of soul and body. The Christian conception of personal immortality may be correct, but I do not *know* that it is so; and yet this lack of

<small>Immortality of the soul.</small>

knowledge will not entail any lowering of my ideals in life. On the contrary, it will in some ways greatly enhance the value of my life to me. The ordinary Christian conception of immortality in some sense shifts the value of life to a sphere beyond death; but, if this life is my only life, then must I make the very best of it, live up to my highest ideals, and see that I do well all that I undertake, for I shall have no opportunity of remedying matters hereafter. In our every-day life if we have little of a thing we appreciate it all the more; and there seems no reason why this should not apply to our own mortality. I will not rashly throw life away or despise it as a mean thing, simply because I do not know that it is to go on for ever. Rather will I feel about it as William Cory (Johnson) expresses himself in "Mimnermus in Church" (a poem in "Ionica") :—

> You promise heavens free from strife,
>   Pure truth, and perfect change of will;
> But sweet, sweet is this human life,
>   So sweet I fain would breathe it still;
> Your chilly stars I can forego,
> This warm kind world is all I know.
>
> You say there is no substance here,
>   One great reality above:
> Back from that void I shrink in fear,
>   And child-like hide myself in love.
> Show me what angels feel : till then,
> I cling, a mere weak man, to men.
>
> You bid me lift my mean desires
>   From faltering lips and fitful veins
> To sexless souls, ideal quires,
>   Unwearied voices, wordless strains:
> My mind with fonder welcome owns
> One dear dead friend's remembered tones.

> Forsooth the present we must give
> To that which cannot pass away;
> All beauteous things for which we live
> By laws of time and space decay.
> But, oh, the very reason why
> I clasp them is because they die.

God. The second conception which we have undertaken to examine is that of God. Most of us, if asked to do this, would find ourselves in some difficulty; but we will get what help we can from a brief historical survey of the growth of the idea. It begins with that earliest theological conception of things which is by now quite familiar to us, and, through a period of animism, very naturally crystallizes, as it were, into a frank anthropomorphism. We saw this ridiculed by Xenophanes, who objected that man, in formulating such a conception, was behaving exactly as lions and cows would, if they had speech, for they would make gods like themselves. We must give up all anthropomorphic ideas and with them the belief in a "personal" god in so far as such a belief is necessarily anthropomorphic. But if a personal god, who is not at the same time anthropomorphic, is a possible conception, then it is one to which we may still hold. "Human personality" is the greatest and the finest thing which we know on this sub-lunary world, and it may well be that some minds can conceive of an analogous "divine" personality. Others will find themselves unable to give any connotation to the word *God* over and above that of the spiritual force in the world which we have seen to be necessarily entailed in our knowledge of the immortality of soul. Some may object that this is far too impersonal a conception; it is something to which they could not pray, and they *know* from experience that they have derived great benefit from prayer. But advanced theologians frankly admit that the greatest benefit of prayer is a psychological one—that peculiar ennobling of the soul which comes from communion with the divine; and psychic things are not yet sufficiently understood by us for even the most hard-headed of intellectualists to deride the idea of any individual soul being "benefited" and strengthened, as it were, by putting itself into contact with the great reservoir of universal soul, much in the same way as Antæus received renewed strength by contact with the earth. Nor is such an impersonal conception necessarily one that takes the warmth entirely out of life. On the contrary, it adds a fresh glow to our ideals; for we realize that it is we ourselves who have to do God's work here on earth. We only know this "spiritual force" as it is manifested in the lives of the human beings around us; we know of no other channels through which it is able to work. And so our co-operation is essential before it can affect anything here; it works in us by inspiring us with lofty ideals, and the more God-like we make ourselves the more easily can we realize those ideals. This, then, must be our endeavour—ἐφ' ὅσον ἐνδέχεται ἀθανατίζειν, which is τὸν θεὸν θεραπεύειν καὶ θεωρεῖν, for it is only so that what κινεῖ ὡς ἐρώμενον can work upon us.

The love of God passeth all understanding.

APPENDIX ON ARISTOTLE'S CRITICISM OF THE PLATONIC IDEAS

THE manner in which Plato spoke of his ideas "things by themselves" (αὐτὰ καθ' αὐτά) inhabiting the celestial region (ὑπερουράνιος τόπος), which was his symbolical way of emphasizing their intellectual and spiritual nature—that they are things of the mind and of the soul, not confined to earth by corporeal limitations—led from the very earliest times to a misunderstanding, much in the same way as the reader of this book might seize upon the phrase "things of the mind" in the above sentence, and exclaim "And so the 'ideas' are *things*, are they? I thought that they were general concepts, universal notions; but now, if you are going to speak of them as *things* I do not know what to make of the doctrine at all, for all *things* are particulars (I can't possibly imagine a *universal thing*); the 'ideas' I had imagined to be, in some sense, the 'explanations' of particular things, but now you make them 'particulars' themselves, and no particular can be explained by another particular." Very much in this way Aristotle, perversely, as it seems to me, thought that Plato "separated" the ideas from phenomena in a manner which reduced them to self-subsisting entities, lying side by side with, or over and above, the phenomena, which they were somehow—it is difficult to see *how*, upon such a supposition—supposed to explain. He could not, or would not, see that Plato spoke of them as χωριστά only in the sense that the "explanation" is separate from the "thing explained," and imagined that such a χωρισμός involved something different from the ἓν εἶδος which Socrates attempted to determine by his universal definitions (τὸ ὁρίζεσθαι καθόλου). This Socratic "definition," which was so like his own τὸ τί ἦν εἶναι, Aristotle appreciated to the full—ἀλλ' ὁ μὲν Σωκράτης τὰ καθόλου οὐ χωριστὰ ἐποίει οὐδὲ τοὺς ὁρισμούς· οἱ δὲ [i.e. the followers of

Plato] ἐχώρισαν καὶ τὰ τοιαῦτα τῶν ὄντων ἰδέας προσηγόρευσαν ("Metaph." 1078b, 30)—but insisted upon taking the χωρισμός of the Platonic ἰδέαι in a sense that reduced them to self-subsisting, "particular" entities. Under this misapprehension, so puerile, it would seem, in a philosopher of his ability, he proceeds to give a detailed attack upon them in the first book of his "Metaphysics":—[1]

> But as for those who posit the Ideas as causes, firstly, in seeking to grasp the causes of the things around us, they introduced others equal in number to these, as if a man who wanted to count things thought he could not do it while they were few, but tried to count them when he had added to their number. For the Forms are practically equal to or not fewer than the things, in trying to explain which these thinkers proceeded from them to the Forms. For to each set of substances there answers a Form which has the same name and exists apart from the substances, and so also in the case of all other groups in which there is one character common to many things, whether the things are in this changeable world or are eternal. Further, of the ways in which we prove that the Forms exist, none is convincing; for from some no inference necessarily follows, and from some it follows that there are Forms of things of which we think there are no Forms. For according to the arguments from the existence of the sciences there will be Forms of all things of which there are sciences, and according to the argument that there is an object for thought even when the thing has perished, there will be Forms of perishable things; for we can have an image of these. Further, of the more accurate arguments, some lead to Ideas of relations, of which we say there is no independent class, and others involve the difficulty of the "third man."[2]

Aristotle goes on to urge a number of other objections to the Ideas, but the whole chapter is so irrelevant as a criticism upon the doctrine as we have described it in Plato himself, that we can only conclude that upon Plato's death his disciples (οἱ περὶ Πλάτωνα) developed the doctrine, under a misapprehension of Plato's real meaning, into a form which rendered it liable to objections of this nature. [It is as one of these later "Platonists" that Aristotle speaks of "we" in the above passage.] This conclusion is confirmed by two considerations: (1) That many points in Aristotle's criticism do not apply to Plato himself, and (2) that Aristotle elsewhere gives a more correct account of the Platonic doctrine.

---

[1] And this in spite of the fact that he recognized ("Metaph." 987a 32) the significance of the Platonic doctrine in providing an answer to the difficulties raised by Cratylus and the Heraclitean flux of things!
[2] "Metaphysics," 990b (translation by Ross).

APPENDIX

(1) The objection that as causes of *de facto* things the Ideas introduce a second class of entities equally numerous with them does not apply to Plato himself. This interpretation is exposed to the "third man" refutation, which is briefly as follows: "The 'third man' is the difficulty known in modern logic as the 'indefinite regress.'. . . It runs thus: If the likeness between Socrates, Plato, and other persons proves that they are all 'copies' of a common archetype, the 'Idea of Man,' then the likeness between this Idea and Socrates must also prove that both Socrates and the Idea are 'copies' of another common archetype, which will be a second and more ultimate Idea of Man; and the likeness between the first and second Ideas of Man proves the existence of a third Idea, which is *their* common archetype, and so on *in indefinitum*. (The real solution of the puzzle is that the relation between Socrates and 'man' is not the same as the relation between Socrates and Plato. Socrates and Plato are both members of the class *men*; 'man' is not a member of the class 'men.'. . .)"[1] So far is Plato's doctrine of ideas from being exposed to such a refutation, that the τρίτος ἄνθρωπος argument is actually taken from him.[2] Again, Aristotle objects that there are sciences of objects for which *the Platonists* themselves do not posit corresponding ideas, e.g. of relatives and of artificial products; but in Plato we do find ideas of these things, e.g. of "bigness" and "equality" in the "Phædo," and in the "Republic" there is the "idea of a bed" ("Repub." 597c).

(2) Aristotle himself elsewhere describes the Platonic doctrine in terms which show a much truer appreciation of it. In chapter six of the first book of his "Metaphysics" he mentions that Socrates was familiar in his youth with Cratylus and the teachings of Heraclitus to the effect that the things of sense are in such a perpetual flux that it is quite impossible for us to have any ἐπιστήμη of them. Socrates himself attempted to find "universals" and "general definitions," but he confined his speculations to the moral sphere. Plato comes next, and he saw that such definitions are impossible in the "sense" sphere. Hence he called things of

---

[1] I take this description from A. E. Taylor's "Aristotle on his Predecessors," p. 119 (note).
[2] "Parmenides," 132; cf. "Republic," 597.

which a κοινὸς ὅρος could be given ἰδέαι, by the side of which αἰσθητά (sensible objects) exist and are called by their several names in virtue of their connexion with these (κατὰ ταῦτα λέγεσθαι). This "connexion" Plato termed μέθεξις :—

> Things of this other sort, then, he called Ideas, and sensible things, he said, were apart from these and were all called after these; for the multitude of things which have the same name as the Form exist by participation in it. Only the name "participation" (μέθεξις) was new; for the Pythagoreans say that things exist by "imitation" (μίμησις) of numbers, and Plato says they exist by participation, changing the name. But what the participation or the imitation of the Forms could be they left an open question.[1]

A few lines farther on Aristotle remarks that the introduction of the doctrine of ideas was due to Plato's logical studies (ἡ τῶν εἰδῶν εἰσαγωγὴ διὰ τὴν ἐν τοῖς λόγοις ἐγένετο σκέψιν), and yet he can go on to interpret the "how" of the μέθεξις, which he says was left "an open question," in a manner which is no contribution to logic at all! This in itself should be sufficient to convince us that his criticisms are directed not against the doctrine of Plato himself—the origin and philosophical bearing of which he here fully appreciates—but against a perversion of that doctrine by the later Platonists of his own age.

[1] "Metaphysics," 987b (translation by Ross).

SOME PHILOSOPHICAL TERMS

Abstract. Separated from matter, practice, or particular examples. An abstract quality is one which does not "exist" alone, but is manifested in many things, as *redness* in a variety of *red objects*. Abstract speculations are concerned with general, or universal, principles, apart from any concrete examples of such principles.

Concept. Idea of a class of objects; general notion or logical abstraction. Psychologists use the word in a more restricted sense than that which it has in this book.

Concrete. The opposite of *abstract*.

Continuous. Without break or interval, such as a line, for example. In its philosophical sense it means that which cannot be divided into parts, and is the opposite of *discrete*.

Cosmology. The science which examines the structure of the universe (κόσμος) in its materialistic aspect.

Deduction. The logical process by which we draw an inference from a general proposition to a particular case, e.g. :—

   (a) *All men are mortal.*
   (b) *Socrates is a man.*
  ∴ (c) *Socrates is mortal.*

In which syllogism, as it is called, (c) is a deduction from (a). It is the opposite of *induction*.

Deductive. The adjective of the above noun.

Discrete. The opposite of *continuous*.

Dynamic. Possessed of power (δύναμις) or latent force. A dynamic conception is one which regards things as containing the possibility of motion or change. It is the opposite of *static*.

Empirical. Based solely on experience (ἐμπειρία) without any "theory" to explain that experience. The knowledge of a quack is empirical, while that of a qualified doctor is scientific.

Entity. That which exists, or has objective existence, as distinguished from its qualities or relations, which may be purely subjective.

Epistemology. The science (λόγος) which examines and explains the possibility and nature of human knowledge (ἐπιστήμη).

Esoteric. Revealed only to the inner few (ἔσω, *within*) who are initiated into mysteries beyond the comprehension of the many; the opposite of *exoteric*.

Ethical. Concerned with morals, treating of moral questions, rules of conduct (ἠθικός relating to character or ἦθος).

Exoteric. The opposite of *esoteric*.

Hedonism. The philosophy according to which pleasure (ἡδονή) is the *summum bonum* of life.

Idealism. The representation of things in ideal form. Contrast, in this sense, *realism*. In philosophy it is the system of thought which gives a higher ideal to human life than that contained in hedonism, and in its explanation of the universe as a whole it takes account of other than material principles. *Subjective* idealism is the system of thought in which the object of external perception is held to consist of ideas.

Induction. The logical process by which we proceed from a number of particular cases to a general rule—ἐπὶ τὰς ἀρχάς, as Aristotle says. From the observation that *this man* has two legs, and *that man* has two legs, and that every individual man whom I have ever seen has two legs, I conclude by induction that *all men* (even those whom I have not seen) have two legs. It is the opposite of *deduction*.

SOME PHILOSOPHICAL TERMS

Logically. Implied, though not necessarily stated, in the nature of the case. *Logically prior* is contrasted with what is prior in *time*, but not in *idea*. In taking a railway journey, for example, my first act *in time* is to go to the station, but my first act *logically* is to decide upon the place to which I want to go. My destination is logically prior to my point of departure.

Materialism. The philosophy which takes account of nothing but matter.

Metaphysics. The science which takes us beyond mere physical or cosmological speculations.

Monism. The doctrine that there is only one principle, or substance, in the universe (μόνος, alone, only).

Objective. External to percipient personality. The opposite of *subjective*.

Phenomena. External objects as they appear to my senses (τὰ φαινόμενα).

Physicist. Student of physics or of natural science in general. In its philosophical sense the word denotes a philosopher who examines the nature (φύσις) of the universe in its materialistic aspect; his science is called *cosmology*.

Pluralism. The opposite of *monism*.

Politics. A much wider term, in philosophy, than in everyday speech. It means the science of the art of government—ἡ πολιτική—and is concerned with the whole *object* of organized communities, and not only with the *means* of carrying out some particular project.

Potential. That which is capable of doing, or being, something; thus a child is potentially an adult, though not *actually* so.

Psychology. The science which examines the human soul (ἡ ψυχή). In ancient times it included speculation upon the whole *nature* of the soul, but in modern speech it is confined to the *workings* of the soul, without involving any theory about its nature.

Qualitatively. In the aspect of possessing a quality; the opposite of *quantitatively*. Thus if I have two sets of six balls, one of wood, and the other of iron, the two sets are quantitatively identical but qualitatively different.

Static. The opposite of *dynamic* (στάσις, standing, station).

Subjective. Belonging to percipient personality; the opposite of *objective*. To make the distinction clear imagine a desert island in the middle of the Pacific, or elsewhere, entirely removed from all percipient life. An explosion takes place on the island. What actually occurs (i.e. the explosion) is objective, but the noise of the explosion is subjective.

Subjectivism. The doctrine that knowledge is merely subjective and can give no criterion of objective truth.

Syllogism. A deductive argument (συλλογή, gathering, collecting). *V. deduction.*

Transcendental. Excelling or surpassing experience; not subject to the limitations of the material universe; often in a spiritual and semi-mystical sense.

INDEX

(A) ENGLISH

Anaxagoras, 39-42.
Anaximander, 15-18.
Anaximenes, 18-20.
Animism, 8.
Anthropomorphism, 9.
"Antigone" of Sophocles, 53.
Aristophanes, 12, 54.
Aristotle, categories of, 140.
— education in, 134.
— criticism of Plato's "Republic," 130.
— — — "Ideas," 144, 159-162.
— the Ethics of, 114-128.
— Logic of, 139-142.
— Metaphysics of, 142-150.
— Politics of, 128-135.
— Psychology of, 135-139.
— Theory of Knowledge, 139-142.
Atomism, 42.

Categories, Aristotelian, 140.
Cause, efficient, 6.
— final, 6.
— formal, 6.
— material, 6.
Conduct, theory of, 54-68.
Copula, the, 29, 49.
Cratylus, 33.

Deduction, 141.
Democracy, 96.
Democritus, 42-44.
Dionysus, 24.

Education, in Aristotle, 134.
Efficient cause, 6.
Eleatic monism, 32-37.

Elements, 17, 19.
Eleusinian mysteries, 24.
Empedocles, 37-39.
Empirical knowledge, 3.
Epictetus, 1.
Epistemology, 104.
Er, myth of, 101.
Euripides, 39.
Euthydemus, 51.
Evolution, 18, 38.

Final cause, 6.
Formal cause, 6.
Freedom, 132.

God, 146, 157.
Gorgias, 48-50.

Heraclitus, 20-22.
Herodotus, 9.
Hesiod, 9.
Homer, 9, 14, 23.
Horace, 26.

Immortality, 10, 100, 126, 155.
Induction, 141.
Involuntary actions, 123.

Justice, 88, 124.
Juvenal, 44.

Knowledge, relativity of, 52.
— scientific, 3, 4.
— theory of, 104.

Leucippus, 42-43.
Lucretius, 38, 44.
Manilius, 151.
Many, and the One, 21, 32, 61, 110.
Material cause, 6.
Materialism, 12, 22.
Miletus, 12.
Monism, 22.
Monotheism, 31.
Motion, 22, 145.
Myths, of Plato, 97-104.

Numbers, doctrine of, 28.

Oligarchy, 96.
One, and the Many, 21, 32, 61, 110.
Orphism, 24.
Ovid, 9, 66.

Parmenides, 32-35.
Pericles, 39.
Philosophy, what it is, 1.
— as *scientia scientiarum*, 5.
— as a way of life, 25.
Plato, 69-112.
— the introductions to the dialogues, 72.
— ideas of, 107-110.
— myths of, 97-104.
— politics of, 92-97.
— psychology of, 88-92.
— "Republic" of, criticized by Aristotle, 130.
Pre-Socratics, 23-44.
Primitive man, 8.
Protagoras, 46-48.
Pythagoras, 25-30.
Pythagorean " pairs," 33.

Reality, 107.
Religion, 11, 152.
Rhetoric, 46, 49.

Scepticism, 9.
Science, 11.
Scientia scientiarum, 5.
Scientific knowledge, 3.
Sensation, theory of, 38.
Socrates, 54-68.
Sophists, 45-53.
Sophocles, " Antigone " of, 53.
Soul, as ἀρχὴ κινήσεως, 100, 136, 145.
— as ἐντελεχεία of body, 136.
— three " parts " of, 89, 137.
Subjectivism, 47, 50, 51.

Thales, 13-15.
Theogony, 9.
Theological conception, 7.
Theology, Olympian, 9.
Thrasymachus, 50.
Timocracy, 96.
Transmigration of souls, 25.
Truth. 5.
Tyranny, 96.

Universals, 4, 143.

Validity, 5.
Virgil, 15, 151.
Virtue, as knowledge, 65.
Voluntary actions, 123.

Xenophanes, 25, 30-32.
Xenophon, 59-60.

Zeno, 35-37.

(B) GREEK

Ἀγαθά, three classes of, 119, 133.
ἀήρ, 18, 19.
αἴσθησις, 2, 137.
αἰσθητά, ἴδια καὶ κοινά, 138.
αἰσθητικὴ ζωή, 118.
τὸ αἰσθητικὸν (μέρος τῆς ψυχῆς), 137.
αἰτίας λογισμός, 87.
αἰτίαι, 6.
ἀκρασία, 66.
ἀναγκαῖον ἐξ ὑποθέσεως, 114, 133.
ἀναίτιος θεός, 101.
ἀνάμνησις, 26, 109.
ἀναπόδεικτοι ἀρχαί, 142.
τὸ ἀντιπεπονθός, 28, 125.
τὸ ἄπειρον, 16.
ἀπόδειξις, 142.
ἀπολαυστικὸς βίος, 27, 115.
ἀπόρροιαι, 38, 43.
ἀραίωσις, 18.
ἀρετή, Aristotle's definition of, 121.
— = ἐπιστήμη, 65.
— as a mean, 121.
— ἠθική, 120.
ἀριστοκρατία, 96, 131.
ἀρχὴ κινήσεως, 6, 100.
ἀρχαί, 6.

Βασιλεία, 131.

Γνῶθι σεαυτόν, 88.
γυμναστική, 134.

Δαιμόνιον Σωκράτους, 57, 62-64.
δημοκρατία, 96, 131.
διαλεκτική, 59.
τὸ διανοητικὸν (μέρος τῆς ψυχῆς), 137.
δικαιοσύνη, 88, 124.

τὸ διότι, 3, 4.
δόξα, ὀρθή, 111.
δυνάμει, 16, 114.
δύναμις, 120.

Ἐθισμός, 120.
εἶδος, 62, 108.
εἰρωνεία (Σωκράτους), 57, 61.
ἔκκρισις, 16.
ἐλευθερία, 122.
ἐμπειρία, 2, 3.
ἐνεργείᾳ, 16, 114.
ἐνέργεια κατ' ἀρετήν, 118.
ἐντελεχεία, 136.
ἕξις, 120.
ἐπαγωγή, 64, 141.
ἐπακτικοὶ λόγοι, 59.
ἐπιθυμία, 89.
ἐπιστήμη, 3, 87, 111.
— = ἀρετή, 65.
ἔρως, as philosophic impulse, 85.
εὐδαιμονία, 116, 118.
εὐσέβεια, 60.

Ἡδονή, 125.
τὸν ἥττω λόγον κρείττω ποιεῖν, 46.

Θεωρητικὸς βίος, 27, 115.
θρεπτικὴ ζωή, 117.
τὸ θρεπτικὸν (μέρος τῆς ψυχῆς), 137.
θυμός, 89.

Ἰδέα, 108.

Καθόλου, τά, 3.
κατηγορίας, σχήματα τῆς, 140.
τὰ κοινῇ κατηγορούμενα, 144.

κρείττονος, τὸ συμφέρον τοῦ, 50.
κρείττω, τὸν ἥττω λόγον ποιεῖν, 46.

Λογισμός, 4.
λογιστικὸν μέρος (τῆς ψυχῆς), 89.

Μαιευτική, 61.
μετεμψύχωσις, see παλιγγενεσία.
μετέχειν (μέθεξις), 108.
μεσότης, 121-123.
μίμημα, 108.
μνήμη, 2.
μουσική, 30, 134.
μῦθος, 97-104.

Νεῖκος, 38.
νόμῳ, 53.
νοῦς (in Anaxagoras), 41.
— παθητικός, 139.

Ὀλιγαρχία, 96, 131.
ὁμοιομερῆ, 41, 43.
ὁρίζεσθαι καθόλου, 59.
τὸ ὅτι, 3, 4.
τὸ οὗ ἕνεκα, 6.
οὐσία, 6.

Παλιγγενεσία, 26, 109.
παράδειγμα, 108.
παρεῖναι, 108.
παρέκβασις, 95, 131.
πόλις, 128.
πολιτεία, 93, 131.
— ὀρθή, 131.
πολιτικὸς βίος, 27, 115.

πράξεις, 53, 120.
προαίρεσις, 121.
πύκνωσις, 18.

Ῥιζώματα, 38.
ῥητορική, 46, 49.

Συλλογισμός, 140.
συμβεβηκός, κατά, 114.
συμφέρον, τοῦ κρείττονος, 50.
συνοικισμός, 102, 128.
σχολή, 126.
σῶμα σῆμα, 100.
σωφροσύνη, 87.

Τέλος, 115.
τέχνη, 2.
τιμοκρατία, 96, 131.
τὸ τί ἦν εἶναι, 6, 143.
τόδε τι, 82, 144.
τοιόνδε τι, 82, 144.
τρίτος ἄνθρωπος, 161.
τύραννις, 96, 131.

ὕλη, 6.
ὑπερουράνιος τόπος, 101, 159.
τὸ ὑποκείμενον, 6.

Φαντασία, 2.
φιλία (Empedoclean), 38.
φύλακες, in Plato's Republic, 93.
φύσει, 53.

Χορηγία, 133.
χωριστός, 144, 159.

For Product Safety Concerns and Information please contact our EU
representative GPSR@taylorandfrancis.com
Taylor & Francis Verlag GmbH, Kaufingerstraße 24, 80331 München, Germany